HUMMUS
& CO.

To all our nieces and nephews, the next generation of amazing cooks (hopefully). No pressure, but we're handing over some of our favourite recipes to you as well as a life lesson: it's not just about the food, but also the laughter, shared table and the people you surround yourself with.

MURDOCH BOOKS

SYDNEY · LONDON

MICHAEL RANTISSI
& KRISTY FRAWLEY

HUMMUS & CO.

MIDDLE EASTERN FOOD
to fall in love with

FOREWORD

WHAT AN HONOUR to be asked to write a few words about this beautiful cookbook that Michael and Kristy have created. It is all about food from the shared table, something that is so important to families both here in Australia and in Israel.

All the planets were in alignment when our daughter Kristy met Michael Rantissi. In March 2007, a day before the 75th birthday of the Sydney Harbour Bridge, the public was given a rare opportunity to walk across this (usually vehicle-clogged) icon. My husband, Peter, and I joined the crowds, crossing the bridge as we made our way into the city. When we flopped into a seat at the Australian Heritage Hotel at The Rocks, we spotted our daughter Kristy with some friends. An introduction to Michael, one of her work colleagues, piqued our curiosity.

After three years working in event management at Le Méridian Hotel in London, Kristy had returned to Australia and found her niche at the idyllic seaside landmark, The Bathers' Pavilion at Balmoral Beach. As office manager and assistant to prominent chef and owner, Serge Dansereau, she wore many hats in her job. One of her roles involved liaising with the kitchen staff, which is how she met Israeli-born Michael—a talented sous chef who'd arrived in Australia after many years spent cooking overseas.

A family holiday to Terrigal in January 2008 was the first time our family experienced Michael's delicious food. In what felt like no time at all, and with minimal ingredients and equipment, Michael created the most amazing lunch for our family. The table was laden with mouth-watering dishes. With this delicious food laid before us, the meal was eaten and enjoyed with a sense of discovery.

From that time on, we regularly encouraged Michael to open his own restaurant to introduce the dining public to the flavours and textures of his food. I am sure this thought had occurred to him before; he just needed things to fall into place, which, in time, they did.

Since then, our family and our friends have been fortunate to share the table at Kristy and Michael's home many times. Their food is always exciting, flavoursome and plentiful. Ingredients such as dukkah, harissa, labne and pomegranate seeds, once so unfamiliar to us, are regularly presented in delicious combinations. Kristy's desserts, often rich and fabulous, always complement the main course so well.

Over the past few years, Kristy and Michael have opened two well-critiqued restaurants, Kepos Street Kitchen and Kepos & Co., as well as their new venture Kepos Catering. Successful life/business partnerships are not accidental; both Kristy and Michael have years of experience in hospitality to draw on, and this has resulted in their shared attention to detail and determination to present healthy, exciting food, served in stylish and contemporary surroundings.

A cookbook is something that usually remains as a permanent fixture on our bookshelf—treasured and beloved. Lots of cookbooks in our home are a bit grubby and tattered from overuse; pages drop out, or are so marked up that the recipe is hard to read. I still have my mother's cookbook from her time at the Domestic Arts School, circa 1926. Those pages are torn and fragile, but, most importantly, they are well-used. There is a common thread when a person wants to share their special recipes and love of food with a reader. It means they are prepared to test their recipes, and even refine and rewrite them if need be. This is a labour of love, just like cooking. We are sure Kristy and Michael will be happy if their cookbooks are beloved, treasured and used, not just shelved.

Looking back, the memorable times are the ones spent around a table, the shared table, with family and friends, and plenty of delicious food.

DIANE AND PETER FRAWLEY

CONTENTS

INTRODUCTION

AS A COUPLE, food runs through everything we do together. It's not unusual for us to plan that night's dinner while we are eating breakfast; our holidays revolve around restaurant bookings and we've been known to read cookbooks in bed. Being able to share this enthusiasm for food in our second book is a wonderful privilege.

MR: Both of us grew up in families where mealtime was very important. For me, growing up in Tel Aviv, my mother would prepare the main meal and serve it late in the afternoon when we came home from school. She'd cook a variety of things, but there was always hummus, some chopped vegetables, at least one or two meat or fish dishes and plenty of salads. Vegetables weren't punishment, they were a reward. Nothing was individually portioned—everyone helped themselves and it was very social and relaxed. This was normal for me. Family dinners for Kristy in Sydney were a little different.

KF: Mum always cooked our meals in the kitchen then plated up there too. She'd serve us at the table and a salad—usually a simple lettuce, tomato, cucumber and mushroom number—would be the only sharing element on the table. The first time Michael ate dinner at my parents' house he found the whole idea of individually portioned meals at a family table surprising. These days, my family love eating with us because they enjoy the sharing table.

MR: Although the food we ate growing up was very different, we both have memories of sitting around the table with our families and discussing our day. On the nights we are able to eat together at home, we usually make a few simple salads, a protein dish and one or two other interesting flavours. Hummus can usually be found on our table—it's a classic that's so versatile.

Our first book, *Falafel for Breakfast*, focused on the signature dishes we served at the restaurant, and how to recreate those at home. The recipes in this book reflect the things Kristy and I make together at home. These are the dishes we love to eat and share with our friends and family—they are simple, tasty and easy to incorporate into all sorts of occasions and meals.

KF: Most of the recipes here are very quick and easy to prepare, but a few take a little more time—we guarantee they are well worth the effort. Don't be put off if an ingredients lists looks long, because once you build up your Mediterranean/Middle Eastern pantry, you only need a few fresh ingredients to throw together a pretty impressive meal.

MR: When I first arrived in Sydney, I found people's perception of Middle Eastern food was either limited or quite far away from the reality. Knowledge of Middle Eastern cuisine didn't extend much further than late-night kebabs or dry falafels, hummus and pita bread. But now there is much more interest so the true nature of this food—the fresh salads, the dips, the spice rubs and the distinctive flavour combinations—is more widely embraced.

The availability of Middle Eastern ingredients has also improved to the point that dishes I grew up eating are now easy for people on this side of the world to make in their homes.

KF: Most, if not all, of these spice blends and ingredients can be found in supermarkets, or at least specialty grocers. Best of all, they aren't expensive and they last a very long time. And if you don't like a particular ingredient or a spice is not to your taste, these recipes can easily be adapted.

MR: Because this book is much more about cooking in the home, versatility is very important. We often swap ingredients depending on what we have in the cupboard or fridge, and that's easily done with many of the recipes. It's more about the feeling of the shared table—celebrating good ingredients in a simple way and bringing people together to enjoy them.

MICHAEL RANTISSI & KRISTY FRAWLEY

CHAPTER ONE

BRUNCH

Brunch is one of our favourite meals because you can really settle in and enjoy yourself—it's never rushed. Not only are brunch recipes usually quick and easy to make, they are also some of the most versatile dishes around. Any of the things in this chapter can easily be eaten for breakfast, a late lunch, a snack or for a quick dinner. Toast with egg and spinach only takes 5 or 10 minutes and makes a very satisfying supper. Steak and eggs is a New York favourite that works anytime of day, and in France you'll often find simple things like a crab omelette on a dinner menu. It's all about perception. Some of these dishes are favourites from our two restaurants, Kepos Street Kitchen and Kepos & Co., and others are recipes we've been cooking for ourselves at home. We hope a few of these become favourites for you, too.

KEPOS BENEDICT

SERVES 4

I know this dish isn't strictly a benedict as it doesn't have the richness of the hollandaise, but you'll love the lightness of it. You can play around with the recipe as required. If you'd like to add a layer of wilted spinach or steamed leek you can. Any vegetables you add will make your day feel slightly healthier.

To make the green tahini, put the parsley, garlic and water in a blender and blitz into as smooth and fine a paste as possible. Add the lemon juice and tahini and blitz again until combined. If the mixture is too thick, add a few more tablespoons of water until it reaches the desired consistency (I like it to have the thickness of hollandaise). Season with salt, to taste.

Poach the eggs so the yolks are still runny, or to your liking.

To assemble, arrange 2 slices of toasted brioche, side by side, on each plate. Top each brioche with 2 slices of smoked salmon, a poached egg and 2–3 tablespoons of green tahini. Top with the salad leaves then sprinkle with freshly ground black pepper, drizzle with olive oil and serve immediately.

NOTE

You can serve any leftover green tahini as a dip.

8 eggs

8 small slices brioche, lightly toasted

16 slices smoked salmon

mixed baby salad leaves, to serve

good-quality olive oil, for drizzling

GREEN TAHINI

2 handfuls flat-leaf (Italian) parsley, coarsely chopped

1 garlic clove

185 ml (6 fl oz/¾ cup) ice-cold water, plus more if needed

3 tablespoons lemon juice

270 g (9½ oz/1 cup) raw tahini

GRANOLA

MAKES 4–6 PORTIONS (ABOUT 600 G/1 LB 5 OZ)

Granola is a great standby breakfast for those mornings you don't have bread or eggs in the house. Once you master the basic recipe, you can be creative and add whatever nuts or seeds you like.

Preheat the oven to 140°C (275°F). Line a large baking tray with baking paper.

Combine the oats, nuts, coconut and seeds in a large bowl.

Combine the sugar, honey and oil in a small saucepan and scrape in the vanilla seeds. Bring to the boil, stirring occasionally. Using a wooden spoon, fold the hot liquid into the oat mixture until evenly combined.

Spread the granola mixture evenly over the prepared baking tray. Bake for 30 minutes, stirring every 5–10 minutes, until the mixture is golden brown.

Remove the granola from the oven and cool to room temperature, stirring every 5 minutes to separate the pieces. Store in an airtight container for up to a week.

NOTE

The quantities can easily be increased to make a bigger batch of granola. You can make it as chunky or as fine as you like. If you prefer a chunkier granola, leave it to cool without stirring.

250 g (9 oz/2½ cups) rolled (porridge) oats
50 g (1¾ oz) pistachios, chopped
30 g (1 oz) raw almonds, chopped
30 g (1 oz) hazelnuts
30 g (1 oz) shredded coconut
30 g (1 oz) pepitas (pumpkin seeds)
30 g (1 oz) sunflower seeds
50 g (1¾ oz) dark brown sugar
75 g (2½ oz) honey
2 tablespoons light olive oil or vegetable oil
1 vanilla bean, split lengthways

BREAKFAST PIDE

MAKES 4

Pide is Turkey's brilliant contribution to any menu, especially brunch. This version can be served at breakfast, lunch or dinner. The filling is up to your taste and imagination—be creative! For best results, use a pizza stone to cook the pide.

Preheat the oven to 250°C (500°F). Place a pizza stone or baking tray in the oven to heat up for at least 1 hour prior to cooking the pide.

Divide the pizza dough into quarters and roll each into a ball. Lightly flour one dough ball all over. Holding the dough with two hands, work around the dough, carefully stretching it lengthways into a long oval shape and taking care not to tear it. Shape the dough so that the centre is thinner than the crust.

Layer the pide with a quarter of the sujuk, cheese and tomato, leaving about 1 cm (½ inch) around the edge of the dough. Crack an egg onto the pide, then break the egg with your fingers and spread it over the top of the pide. Season with salt and freshly ground black pepper. Roll in the edges of the dough to form a lip, then pinch the edges of the dough together at each pointy end to seal it, leaving some of the filling exposed.

Carefully put the pide onto the hot pizza stone or baking tray. Bake for about 3–5 minutes, until the edge of the pide is coloured and the base is cooked. Check that the bottom is cooked by lifting it up with a pair of tongs. Transfer the cooked pide to a plate and repeat with the remaining dough and toppings.

NOTE

I recommend making each pide just before you put it in the oven, rather than preparing all four at once and leaving them to sit while the others are cooking.

Pictured on page 22

½ quantity pizza dough (page 242)
plain (all-purpose) flour, for dusting
400 g (14 oz) sujuk sausage, chopped
200 g (7 oz) grated mozzarella cheese
2 tomatoes, chopped
4 eggs

ASPARAGUS, PEA AND FETA TART

SERVES 6

I think a weekend brunch is sometimes the best meal of the week because you have a little more time to prepare and a little more time to enjoy the meal. I don't get to have brunch that often at the moment because I'm usually cooking for other people at the restaurants, but it's a great way to entertain friends and family. This tart is easy to assemble and most of the components can be made ahead of time. It looks pretty and tastes delicious and fresh. If you don't want to use peas you can use another vegetable.

Preheat the oven to 190°C (375°F). Line a large baking tray with baking paper.

Put the peas in a bowl and crush them. Stir in the lemon zest, lemon juice and 3 tablespoons of the olive oil. Season with salt and freshly ground black pepper and set aside.

Put the pastry on the prepared tray and bake for about 20 minutes, or until golden brown, puffed up and very firm. Remove from the oven and set aside to cool to room temperature.

Heat a chargrill pan or a barbecue grill plate to high. Drizzle the asparagus with 1 tablespoon of the olive oil and sprinkle with salt and freshly ground black pepper. Cook for 1–2 minutes, until grill marks appear.

To assemble the tart, put the pastry on a serving board or chopping board (this will make the tart easier to cut) and top with the crushed pea mixture. Crumble the feta evenly over the tart. Tear the eggs in half and arrange them on the tart. Top with the grilled asparagus and sprinkle with sea salt and cracked black pepper. Drizzle with olive oil and scatter over micro herbs, if using.

NOTE

The pastry has a long cooking time. Once cut, it needs to be able to hold its shape and soak up the juices.

350 g (12 oz/2½ cups) frozen peas, thawed overnight

grated zest and juice of 1 lemon

4 tablespoons olive oil, plus extra for drizzling

1 sheet store-bought all-butter puff pastry, about 20 x 30 cm (8 x 12 inches)

12–14 asparagus spears, peeled and trimmed

150 g (5½ oz) feta cheese

3 soft-boiled eggs

micro herbs, to garnish (optional)

BAKED EGGS WITH SPINACH AND SUMAC

SERVES 6

Shakshuka (eggs baked in a spiced sauce) is a great go-to brunch dish and an all-time favourite with many variations. This is a Turkish version, which uses cream instead of a spicy tomato and pepper sauce. You can definitely substitute any other greens you like for the spinach, such as kale, silverbeet (Swiss chard) or cavolo nero. If you want a stronger cheese flavour, add a handful of grated haloumi or several dollops of ricotta or goat's cheese.

Preheat the oven to 190°C (375°F).

Heat the oil in an ovenproof frying pan over medium heat. Sauté the onion and garlic for 5 minutes, or until translucent but not coloured. Add the chopped spinach and cook until wilted, about 2 minutes. Stir in the cream, sugar, sumac and nutmeg. Season with salt and freshly ground black pepper.

Gently crack the eggs into the sauce, spacing them evenly around the pan, and bake for about 10 minutes, or until the eggs are done to your liking. After 8 minutes the eggs will be very runny; after 10 minutes they will be a bit firmer; and after 15 minutes they will be well-done.

To serve, crumble the goat's cheese over the eggs and sprinkle with the chilli and extra sumac.

4 tablespoons olive oil

1 small brown onion, chopped

2 garlic cloves, crushed

1½ bunches English spinach, coarsely chopped

4 tablespoons thickened (whipping) cream

1 tablespoon caster (superfine) sugar

1 tablespoon ground sumac, plus extra for sprinkling

¼ teaspoon freshly grated nutmeg

6 eggs

100 g (3½ oz) goat's cheese

1 small fresh red chilli, finely chopped

CAULIFLOWER FRITTERS

SERVES 4

Fritters are a great alternative to toast in the morning. The batter can be made in advance—just bring it to room temperature before you start to cook the fritters. This gluten-free recipe is made using chickpea flour.

Preheat the oven to 180°C (350°F). Line a large baking tray with baking paper.

Toss the cauliflower, 100 ml (3½ fl oz) of the oil and the cumin together in a large bowl. Transfer the cauliflower to the baking tray and bake for 35–40 minutes, until tender. Using a fork, lightly mash the cauliflower, then set aside to cool to room temperature.

Transfer the cooled cauliflower to a bowl and mix with the eggs, chickpea flour, parsley, chilli and sumac until well combined. Fold the crumbled goat's cheese through the batter.

Heat the remaining oil in a non-stick frying pan over medium heat. Spoon 3 tablespoons of the mixture into the pan to make each fritter. Cook the fritters in batches for 2–3 minutes on each side, until golden.

500 g (1 lb 2 oz) cauliflower florets (not too small)

140 ml (4½ fl oz) olive oil

1 tablespoon ground cumin

4 eggs

70 g (2½ oz) chickpea flour (besan)

2 large handfuls flat-leaf (Italian) parsley, finely chopped

1 large fresh green chilli, finely chopped

1 tablespoon ground sumac

150 g (5½ oz) goat's cheese, crumbled

MEATBALLS WITH EGGS AND LABNEH

SERVES 4–6

This recipe combines two of my favourite things: meatballs and shakshuka (see page 20), and even includes some creamy labneh. This version of shakshuka is made with the more traditional tomato base. You can add crème fraîche or sour cream instead of labneh, but I find it a lighter option if you are serving this dish for brunch.

Put the beef, egg and breadcrumbs in a large bowl. Season with some salt and freshly ground black pepper and use your hands to combine. Roll 1 tablespoon of mixture into a ball, then repeat until all of the mixture is used up. Set aside.

Heat the oil in a frying pan over medium heat and sauté the onion and garlic for 3–4 minutes. Add the tomatoes and stock, bring to the boil and cook for 5 minutes, then add the meatballs and simmer for about 30–35 minutes. Add the spices, season with additional salt and black pepper and cook for a further 5 minutes.

Transfer the meatballs and sauce to a large deep frying pan. Crack the eggs into the sauce, spacing them evenly around the pan, but don't stir. Cook over medium heat for 4–5 minutes, or until the eggs are done to your liking. Remove the pan from the heat.

Dollop the labneh onto the meatballs and sauce. Garnish with the coriander, a little black pepper and a drizzle of olive oil.

NOTE

Lightly oil your hands when rolling the meatballs to give them a smooth finish.

Pictured on page 22

300 g (10½ oz) minced (ground) beef

1 egg, lightly beaten

4 tablespoons dry breadcrumbs

3 tablespoons olive oil, plus extra for drizzling

1 brown onion, finely diced

2 garlic cloves, crushed

400 g (14 oz) tin chopped tomatoes

200 ml (7 fl oz) chicken stock

2 tablespoons sweet paprika

1 tablespoon ground cumin

1 tablespoon ground coriander

8 eggs

4 tablespoons labneh

coriander (cilantro) sprigs, to garnish

SIRLOIN, EGGS AND RAS EL HANOUT

SERVES 4

On my last visit to New York, I went to a great restaurant called Prune for a weekend brunch. One dish on the menu was steak and eggs. This recipe is my take on that very classic American dish. The sprinkle of ras el hanout, a spice blend that gives so many Middle Eastern dishes their distinctive flavour, gives this a completely different personality. To make it just that little bit more special, why not serve it with a mimosa?

Pat the steaks dry and sprinkle with the ras el hanout and sea salt.

Heat the oil in a non-stick frying pan over high heat. Sear the steaks for 2 minutes, then flip and sear for another 2 minutes, then flip and sear for another minute on each side. Add the butter to the pan and cook the steaks for 30 seconds to 1 minute, basting them with the butter. Remove the steaks from the pan and set aside to rest.

Add the eggs to the pan and fry them in the pan juices until they are done to your liking.

To serve, put a fried egg on top of each steak. Sprinkle with the cumin, season with freshly ground black pepper and then top with some chopped parsley.

4 x 200 g (7 oz) sirloin (New York) steaks

2 teaspoons ras el hanout

sea salt flakes

3 tablespoons olive oil

40 g (1½ oz) butter

4 eggs

½ teaspoon ground cumin

2 tablespoons chopped flat-leaf (Italian) parsley

CHOPPED LIVER SPREAD

SERVES 6-8

If you are a big fan of chicken liver pâté, this spread is a lovely cheat's version. It takes minimum effort but delivers maximum impact, and it's bulletproof. Spread it over crisp bread or toast with a side of pickles for a delicious brunch dish. It also makes great finger food.

Heat 50 ml (1½ fl oz) of the oil in a large frying pan over medium heat. Cook the onion for 5–7 minutes, until caramelised and golden brown. Transfer to a bowl and set aside.

Reheat the frying pan over high heat and cook the chicken livers in two batches for about 2 minutes on each side, or until browned on the outside and still quite soft and pink on the inside.

Put the chicken livers, caramelised onion, eggs, mustard, crushed cumin seeds and remaining oil in a food processor and blend until the mixture forms a paste that is almost smooth. Season with salt and freshly ground black pepper, then fold in the chives.

The spread can be served as soon as it is made, or stored in an airtight container in the fridge for up to 5 days.

NOTE

You can cook the chicken livers for longer if you prefer them more cooked, but it will change the colour and consistency of the spread.

160 ml (5¼ fl oz) olive oil

2 small brown onions, sliced

500 g (1 lb 2 oz) chicken livers, trimmed

3 hard-boiled eggs

1 tablespoon wholegrain mustard

½ teaspoon cumin seeds, toasted and crushed

30 g (1 oz) chives, chopped

SARDINE AND CORIANDER PIZZA

MAKES 4

I know that sardine pizza may not sound like the most appealing dish, but fresh, seasonal sardines are sweet and delicious, and also very cost effective. The coriander paste takes away a little of that strong fishy flavour that turns some people off, although that is what I love about them. You can cook any leftover sardines on the barbecue, or pickle them.

Preheat the oven to 250°C (500°F). Place a pizza stone or baking tray in the oven to heat up at least 1 hour prior to cooking the pizza.

Put the chopped coriander and garlic in a food processor and blitz for 30 seconds. Add the grated cheese and almond meal and blend for 2 minutes, or until the mixture forms a paste. Add the oil, lemon zest and juice, and salt, to taste, and blend until the mixture is combined. It should look like pesto and have a similar consistency. Set aside.

Divide the pizza dough into quarters and roll each into a ball. Lightly flour one dough ball all over. Holding the dough with two hands, work around the dough, carefully stretching it in a circular motion and taking care not to tear it. Shape the dough so that the centre is thinner than the crust.

Spread 2–3 tablespoons of the coriander paste over the pizza base, leaving a 1 cm (½ inch) border. Arrange 4 of the butterflied sardines, cut side down, on top. Scatter a few slices of red onion over the sardines.

Carefully put the pizza onto the hot pizza stone or baking tray. Bake for 3–5 minutes, until the edge of the pizza is coloured and the base is cooked. Transfer the cooked pizza to a plate and repeat with the remaining dough, coriander paste, sardines and red onion.

Drizzle each pizza with some good-quality olive oil and garnish with coriander leaves.

NOTE

For best results, use a pizza stone. If you don't have a pizza stone, you can use a baking tray. I suggest assembling each pizza just before you put it in the oven, rather than preparing all four at once and leaving them to sit while the others are cooking.

1 large handful coriander (cilantro), chopped, plus extra leaves to garnish

2 garlic cloves

2 tablespoons grated haloumi or parmesan cheese

2 tablespoons almond meal

3 tablespoons olive oil, plus extra for drizzling

zest and juice of ½ lemon

½ quantity pizza dough (page 242)

plain (all-purpose) flour, for dusting

16 fresh sardines, filleted and butterflied

1 red onion, thinly sliced

LAMB PIZZA

MAKES 4

Nothing speaks of my childhood more than this Middle Eastern style pizza, 'bil ajin' (dough and meat). Junk food and fast-food chains were just beginning to appear in Tel Aviv when I was growing up. Of course, being kids we wanted to try all the new food, but my mum was still a bit old-fashioned and insisted on cooking every day. Instead of takeaways, she would create recipes that were Middle Eastern interpretations of Western food—that was her way of selling it to us. It always worked. Thanks, Mum!

Preheat the oven to 250°C (500°F). Place a pizza stone or baking tray in the oven to heat up at least 1 hour prior to cooking the pizza.

Heat the oil in a frying pan over medium heat and sauté the onion for 3–5 minutes. Increase the heat to high, add the lamb and cook, stirring and breaking up the lumps, for 5 minutes. Stir the chermoula through the lamb and cook for 1 minute, without cooking the lamb all the way through.

Divide the pizza dough into quarters and roll each into a ball. Lightly flour one dough ball all over. Holding the dough with both hands, work around the dough, carefully stretching it in a circular motion and taking care not to tear it. Shape the dough so that the centre is thinner than the crust.

Spread a quarter of the lamb mixture over the pizza base. Carefully put the pizza onto the hot pizza stone or baking tray and bake for 3–5 minutes, until the edge of the pizza is coloured and the base is cooked. Transfer the cooked pizza to a plate. Repeat with the remaining dough and lamb mixture.

Drizzle each pizza with some good-quality olive oil and top with a few dollops of Greek-style yoghurt or labneh, some toasted pine nuts and mint leaves.

NOTES

For best results, use a pizza stone. If you don't have a pizza stone, you can use a baking tray. I suggest assembling each pizza just before you put it in the oven, rather than preparing all four at once and leaving them to sit while the others are cooking.

3 tablespoons olive oil, plus extra for drizzling

1 brown onion, finely chopped

600 g (1 lb 5 oz) minced (ground) lamb

3 tablespoons chermoula (page 225)

½ quantity pizza dough (page 242)

plain (all-purpose) flour, for dusting

Greek-style yoghurt or labneh, to serve

toasted pine nuts, to serve

mint leaves, to garnish

ZUCCHINI, SUJUK AND LABNEH OMELETTE

MAKES 4

Excellent served for brunch or even a Sunday night dinner, this dish, which sits somewhere between an omelette and a frittata, is so easy to make. I don't think we celebrate the versatility of eggs enough—they are quick to prepare, nutritious and so much more than a breakfast food. The main ingredient in this dish is zucchini—and it may seem that there is a lot of it, but it helps to give the omelette its light, fluffy texture. The sujuk sausage adds a salty, spicy kick.

Put the grated zucchini in a bowl and sprinkle with the salt. Set aside until the zucchini releases its juices, about 15 minutes. Drain the zucchini, return to the bowl and set aside.

Preheat the oven to 180°C (350°F).

Heat 2 tablespoons of the olive oil in a 24 cm (9½ inch) ovenproof frying pan over medium–high heat. Fry the sujuk until crisp, then transfer to a plate and set aside. Leave the excess oil in the pan to cook the omelette.

Add the eggs, labneh, chopped parsley and half the crispy sujuk to the zucchini. Season with freshly ground black pepper and whisk to combine.

Reheat the frying pan over medium heat. Pour in the egg mixture and cook for 2–3 minutes, then transfer the pan to the oven and cook for 10 minutes, or until the omelette is done to your liking.

While the omelette is cooking, put the remaining crispy sujuk, mixed herbs, pine nuts, lemon juice and remaining olive oil in a bowl and toss to combine.

Flip the cooked omelette onto a plate and serve topped with dollops of labneh and the sujuk and herb mixture.

800 g (1 lb 12 oz) zucchini (courgettes), about 4 in total, coarsely grated

1 tablespoon salt

100 ml (3½ fl oz) olive oil

200 g (7 oz) sujuk sausage, diced

4 eggs

2 tablespoons labneh, plus 4 tablespoons extra to serve

3 tablespoons chopped flat-leaf (Italian) parsley

2 large handfuls mixed herbs, such as chives, flat-leaf (Italian) parsley, mint and coriander (cilantro), leaves picked

70 g (2½ oz) pine nuts, toasted

juice of ½ lemon

GREEN PEA AND RICOTTA FRITTERS

MAKES 14–16

These fritters are quite versatile as they can be served for breakfast or brunch with eggs, bacon, salmon, ham or any other cold meat. At lunchtime they could be served as a side dish with a piece of steak. You can also use the mixture to make one large fritter and cut it into wedges to serve. I prefer using frozen peas in this recipe even when fresh peas are available because I find them creamier. They are also always on hand in the freezer, which makes these an easy choice in the morning when I'm deciding what to cook.

Put the peas in a food processor and blend until lightly crushed.

Heat 3 tablespoons of the oil in a frying pan over medium heat. Sauté the onion and garlic until transparent, then set aside to cool.

Add the peas, sautéed onion and garlic, eggs, flour, fresh and dried mint to a large bowl and mix to combine. Season with salt and freshly ground black pepper. Fold in the ricotta in chunks, trying not to break it up too much.

Heat the remaining 2 tablespoons of oil in a non-stick frying pan over medium heat. Spoon 3 tablespoons of the mixture into the pan to make each fritter. Cook the fritters in batches for 2–3 minutes on each side, or until lightly golden.

500 g (1 lb 2 oz) frozen peas, thawed

100 ml (3½ fl oz) olive oil

1 small brown onion, finely diced

2 garlic cloves, crushed

4 small eggs

60 g (2¼ oz) plain (all-purpose) flour

1 large handful mint leaves, finely chopped

1 tablespoon dried mint

200 g (7 oz) ricotta cheese

FISH BURGERS WITH ZUCCHINI AND DILL SALAD

MAKES 4 BURGERS

A lot of home cooks are intimidated by cooking fish. This is an easy recipe to start practising your fish-cooking skills. The burgers make an amazing weekend treat to serve at any time of day, not just at brunch.

Put the minced fish, egg, breadcrumbs, parsley, lemon zest, chilli flakes and olive oil in a large bowl and season with salt and freshly ground black pepper. Use your hands to combine the mixture and knead it for 1–2 minutes. Divide the mixture into 4 balls and shape each into a patty. Set aside in the fridge until ready to use.

To make the salad, combine the zucchini, oil, lemon juice, dill and capers in a bowl and season with salt and pepper.

Heat the barbecue grill plate to medium–high. Cook the fish patties for 2–3 minutes on each side, or until done to your liking.

Lightly toast the insides of the brioche buns. Spoon the mayonnaise onto the bun bases. Add some salad and a fish patty, then add more salad and finish with the bun tops.

NOTE

My preferred method of mincing the fish is using an electric mixer with a mincer attachment. Otherwise, use a sharp knife to dice the fish as finely as possible.

700 g (1 lb 9 oz) skinless, boneless snapper fillets, minced (see Note)

1 egg

3 tablespoons dry breadcrumbs

3 tablespoons chopped flat-leaf (Italian) parsley

grated zest of 1 lemon

1 teaspoon chilli flakes

3 tablespoons olive oil

4 brioche buns, cut in half

4 tablespoons good-quality whole-egg mayonnaise

ZUCCHINI AND DILL SALAD

2 small zucchini (courgettes), thinly sliced

3 teaspoons olive oil

juice of 1 lemon

1 small handful dill

2 tablespoons capers, rinsed

FIGS WITH BURRATA AND PROSCIUTTO

SERVES 4–6 AS A STARTER

This dish is all about celebrating simplicity and letting the flavours of these special ingredients shine. I prefer pomegranate molasses to caramelised balsamic vinegar, as it is less acidic and it adds a complex yet harmonious flavour. Use a large, flat serving platter to assemble and serve the dish.

Place the burrata balls on a large serving platter. Add the fig halves and the prosciutto, arranging the ingredients in an uneven way. Drizzle the pomegranate molasses and olive oil over the top. Sprinkle with the basil leaves, black salt and freshly cracked black pepper.

4 x 100 g (3½ oz) or 2 x 200 g (7 oz) burrata cheese balls, drained

6 fresh figs, halved lengthways

100 g (3½ oz) sliced prosciutto

3 tablespoons pomegranate molasses

100 ml (3½ fl oz) olive oil

10 basil leaves

black salt, to serve

DUKKAH EGG SALAD

SERVES 4

Egg salad made with mayonnaise is a classic, but this version is a much more interesting alternative. There's a nice spicy kick from the chillies and a great acidity from the gherkins. It works really well as a breakfast dish or as part of a brunch meal, and is delicious on rye bread.

Peel the eggs and break them into about four chunks each. Add them to a bowl with the remaining ingredients and gently fold to combine.

NOTE

Use pickled jalapeño chillies if you can find them.

Pictured on page 22

8 soft-boiled eggs

100 g (3½ oz) dukkah

15 g (½ oz/½ cup) dill, stems removed

50 g (1¾ oz) pickled chillies, coarsely chopped

100 g (3½ oz) gherkins (pickles), coarsely chopped

100 ml (3½ fl oz) olive oil

ZUCCHINI AND ZA'ATAR EMPANADA

MAKES 6–8 SLICES

Zucchini is a completely underrated vegetable, and I use it in many different recipes as it is available all year round. If you are not a zucchini fan, use another vegetable to make the filling for this traditional South American pie.

To make the dough, put the flour, sea salt flakes and sugar in a food processor and blitz for a few seconds to combine. Add the butter and yoghurt and blitz until almost combined. Form the dough into a ball, wrap in plastic wrap and refrigerate for 2 hours.

While the dough is resting, make the filling. Cut the zucchini into 2–3 mm ($\frac{1}{16}$–$\frac{1}{8}$ inch) thick slices. Coat with the olive oil and season with salt and freshly ground black pepper. Heat a barbecue grill plate or chargrill pan to high. Cook the zucchini for 1 minute on each side (do not overcook it as it will cook further in the oven).

Transfer the zucchini to a bowl and gently fold in the pine nuts, feta, za'atar or oregano leaves and lemon zest. Taste and add extra seasoning if needed—be careful with the salt as the feta is salty and the zucchini has already been seasoned. Set aside to cool to room temperature.

Preheat the oven to 180°C (350°F). Line a large baking tray with baking paper.

Divide the dough in half and roll out on a lightly floured surface to make two circles, one about 24 cm (9½ inches) for the base and one about 28 cm (11¼ inches) for the top of the pie. The dough for the top will be slightly thinner than the base.

Put the smaller dough circle on the baking tray and mound the filling in the centre, leaving a 2 cm (¾ inch) border around the edge. Brush the beaten egg around the edge of the base. Place the larger dough circle on top and press the edges together using a fork to seal it. Score the top into wedges and cut a small hole in the centre of the dough to release the steam during cooking. Brush the top with beaten egg and bake for 25–30 minutes, until golden.

Pictured on page 70

DOUGH

500 g (1 lb 2 oz/3⅓ cups) plain (all-purpose) flour, plus extra for rolling

2 teaspoons sea salt flakes

1 tablespoon sugar

250 g (9 oz) butter, at room temperature

250 g (9 oz) Greek-style yoghurt

1 egg, beaten

FILLING

5 small firm zucchini (courgettes)

3 tablespoons olive oil

70 g (2½ oz) pine nuts, lightly toasted

150 g (5½ oz) Danish feta cheese, crumbled

1 handful za'atar or oregano leaves

grated zest of 1 lemon

REUBEN SANDWICH

SERVES 4

These sandwiches are great to make when you're having a group of family or friends over as the recipe can easily be increased to feed a crowd. To save time, toast the bread separately and serve a deconstructed version of the sandwiches with all the ingredients on the table so your guests can assemble their own.

Put the mayonnaise, Worcestershire and Tabasco sauces in a small bowl. Mix to combine and season with salt and freshly ground black pepper. Set aside.

Heat a chargrill pan or a barbecue grill plate to medium–high. Using a pastry brush, brush one side of a slice of rye bread with olive oil. On the other side, place a dollop of the mayonnaise mixture, a slice of cheese, 3 slices of corned beef, a few tablespoons of sauerkraut and another slice of cheese. Top with a slice of bread then brush the top with olive oil. Repeat to make 4 sandwiches in total.

Cook the sandwiches for a few minutes on each side or until grill marks appear and the bread is coloured to your liking. Carefully turn the sandwiches over and cook the other side.

120 g (4¼ oz/½ cup) good-quality whole-egg mayonnaise

1 teaspoon Worcestershire sauce

1 teaspoon Tabasco sauce

8 slices rye bread

4 tablespoons olive oil

8 slices kashkaval cheese

12 slices corned beef (see below)

100 g (3½ oz) sauerkraut

CORNED BEEF

SERVES 10–12

Corned beef is a great example of a recipe that takes minimum effort and delivers maximum impact. It may sound complicated, but cooking a secondary cut of meat with some aromatics for a few hours is really one of the simplest things you can do. Why buy it when you can exercise your culinary talents and satisfy your palate by making it yourself?

Put the silverside in a large saucepan. Add the peeled whole onion and garlic cloves, bay leaves, peppercorns and enough cold water to cover the silverside. Bring to the boil over medium heat. Reduce the heat to medium–low and simmer for 2½–3 hours, or until soft. Top up the water as needed and skim the surface occasionally, being careful not to remove the aromatics. Leave the corned beef to cool in the liquid.

Drain and thinly slice the cooled corned beef. Store in the fridge for 5–7 days.

1.2–1.5 kg (2 lb 11 oz–3 lb 5 oz) piece silverside

1 large onion

2 garlic cloves

2 bay leaves

6 black peppercorns

Reuben sandwich

SPINACH AND PINE NUT ROLLS

MAKES 10

When I was growing up, these vegetable rolls were another form of the traditional bourekas—a savoury pastry. They are filling on their own, but also really good with something light, like a green salad, if it's closer to lunch time. The rolls can be made in advance, sliced and frozen, ready to be baked at a later date when you don't feel like cooking.

Coarsely chop the leaves and stems of the English spinach. Bring a large saucepan of salted water to the boil. Blanch the spinach for 30 seconds, then drain and refresh in icy cold water. Squeeze out any excess liquid, then set aside.

Heat the olive oil in a large frying pan over medium heat. Sauté the onion and garlic for 3–4 minutes, until transparent but not coloured. Transfer to a bowl and set aside to cool to room temperature.

Mix the spinach into the onion and garlic and season with the chilli flakes, salt and freshly ground black pepper.

Place a sheet of pastry on a lightly floured surface then divide into four 30 cm (12 inch) squares. Spread the spinach mixture over the pastry, leaving a 2 cm (¾ inch) strip free along one edge. Sprinkle the pine nuts and feta over the spinach. Brush the empty pastry strip with the beaten egg and then, starting at the opposite side, firmly roll up the pastry into a roulade. Don't roll it so tightly that the mixture squeezes out. Repeat with the other pastry sheets.

Preheat the oven to 180°C (350°F). Line a large baking tray with baking paper.

Using a serrated knife, cut the roulade into 10 equal pieces. Place on the baking tray (do not overcrowd the tray as the rolls will double in size). Bake the rolls for 18–20 minutes, or until the pastry is golden brown. Remove the tray from the oven and use a pastry brush to glaze the rolls with the extra olive oil. Set the rolls aside to cool slightly before serving warm.

NOTE

It is important to use a serrated knife to cut the roulade in order to give a clean cut that will allow the pastry to puff up.

400 g (14 oz/2 bunches) English spinach

4 tablespoons olive oil, plus 3 tablespoons extra, for glazing

1 small brown onion, finely chopped

3 garlic cloves, crushed

½ teaspoon chilli flakes

4 store-bought all-butter puff pastry sheets

plain (all-purpose) flour, for rolling

100 g (3½ oz/⅔ cup) pine nuts, toasted

200 g (7 oz) feta cheese, crumbled

1 egg, lightly beaten

STRAWBERRY AND ROSE PETAL JAM

FILLS A 1 LITRE (35 FL OZ/4 CUP) JAR

When strawberries are in season, in spring and summer, they're readily available and very affordable. This is a great time to make this beautiful jam. Rose petals and rosewater give it a full flavour and a bit of a twist from a standard strawberry jam.

Wash the strawberries and cut off the green tops. Cut the strawberries in half, put them in a large saucepan and lightly crush them using a potato masher. Stir in the sugar.

Cook the strawberries over low heat for 20 minutes, stirring every few minutes so the mixture does not catch. Crush the strawberries again.

Stir in the rose petals, rosewater, lemon zest and lemon juice. Increase the heat to medium and boil the mixture for 5 minutes, skimming the surface if needed.

Spoon the jam into a large sterilised jar or several smaller jars and seal. The unopened jam will keep for 6 months. Once opened, store in the fridge for up to 1 month.

1 kg (2 lb 4 oz) fresh or frozen strawberries

750 g (1 lb 10 oz) jam setting sugar

3 tablespoons edible dried rosebuds or rose petals

2 tablespoons rosewater

grated zest and juice of ½ lemon

DATE, CLOVE
AND ALMOND JAM

FILLS A 1.2 LITRE (42 FL OZ) JAR

There are jams that are for toast and then there are jams that can be used as a filling when baking, or as a topping for ice cream. This one works in all of those ways. My aunty used to make a jam with unripened dates. This is a cheat's version of that jam, but equally delicious.

Put the dates, sugar, cloves and 500 ml (17 fl oz/2 cups) water in a saucepan and cook over medium heat for 10 minutes. The dates should start to break down. Add the almonds and another 500 ml (17 fl oz/2 cups) water. Reduce the heat to low and cook the jam for 10 minutes, stirring occasionally so it doesn't catch.

Spoon the jam into a large sterilised jar or several smaller jars and seal. Allow to cool, then store in the fridge for up to 1 month.

1 kg (2 lb 4 oz) medjool dates, pitted and halved
500 g (1 lb 2 oz) caster (superfine) sugar
5 cloves
200 g (7 oz/1¼ cups) blanched whole almonds

TOMATO BAHARAT JAM

FILLS A 1 LITRE (35 FL OZ/4 CUP) JAR

'Baharat' means spice, and this gently spiced jam is halfway between a jam and a relish, which definitely doubles its uses. It's a great condiment to serve with pâté or cold cuts. We always have a jar of it in our fridge at home and love it on bacon and egg rolls for an extra kick of flavour.

Cut a cross in the base of each tomato. Plunge the tomatoes into a bowl of boiling water for 1 minute, then transfer to a bowl of iced water. Drain and peel the tomatoes. Cut in half, discarding the seeds, and chop the flesh.

Put the tomato, sugar, star anise, cloves and cinnamon sticks in a large saucepan. Cook over medium heat, stirring occasionally, for 25 minutes. Reduce the heat to low, add the tomato paste and cook, stirring occasionally, for 20 minutes, or until thickened. Add the lemon juice, sea salt and freshly ground black pepper, to taste. Cook for a further 5 minutes.

Spoon the jam into a large sterilised jar or several smaller jars and seal. Allow to cool, then store in the fridge for up to 2 weeks. Remove the star anise, cloves and cinnamon sticks before serving.

600 g (1 lb 5 oz) tomatoes

200 g (7 oz) caster (superfine) sugar

3 star anise

2 cloves

4 cinnamon sticks

2 teaspoons tomato paste (concentrated purée)

juice of ½ lemon

1 teaspoon sea salt flakes

CHAPTER TWO

SALADS

When Michael and I first started dating, I used to make something he called a 'Kiki salad'. It included pretty much every ingredient from the veg aisle: lettuce, rocket, capsicums, tomatoes, cucumber, mushrooms ... Michael soon convinced me that simpler was better. He taught me that a salad should be something that was thoughtfully put together, not a collection of what was in the fridge. I'm definitely a convert (though very occasionally I'll sneak a Kiki salad in, for old times' sake).

Michael believes in finding the most beautiful ingredient—a tomato or beetroot, for example—and then making that the hero by preparing it simply and dressing it with a few other things that bring out its beautiful flavours. The salads here feature simple ingredients and can be eaten as side dishes with your main course, or as a meal on their own. They also make excellent lunches, if you take yours to work.

WHITE BEAN AND SUMAC SALAD

SERVES 8 AS A SIDE DISH

To me, a salad should venture beyond cold chopped vegetables. It should have different textures, contrasting flavours and include something special that makes you want to go back for another helping. This is a light and refreshing dish that goes well with meat or fish. The lemon juice and sumac give it a lovely zing.

Put the dried beans in a large bowl and cover with 1.25 litres (44 fl oz/ 5 cups) water. Leave to soak for at least 12 hours, but ideally overnight.

Drain the beans and lightly rinse under cold running water. Transfer to a large saucepan with plenty of cold water and cook over medium-low heat for 1½ hours, or until the beans are tender but not mushy. Drain and allow to cool completely.

Transfer the cooled beans to a large bowl and add the remaining ingredients. Season with salt and freshly ground black pepper and gently mix until combined, trying not to break up the beans.

NOTE

You can also substitute two 400 g (14 oz) tins of cannellini beans for the dried beans. Simply drain them and mix with the other salad ingredients.

195 g (7 oz/1 cup) dried cannellini beans

1 large red onion, thinly sliced

1 large handful parsley, leaves coarsely chopped

1 large handful coriander (cilantro), leaves coarsely chopped

1½ large fresh red chillies, thinly sliced

3 tablespoons sumac

125 ml (4 fl oz/½ cup) olive oil

juice of 1 lemon

BEETROOT AND SALMON SALAD

SERVES 4–6 AS A SIDE DISH

The beetroot and salmon really complement each other, and once the roasting is done this is so quick to assemble. Serve this salmon salad on croutons with good-quality mayonnaise for fantastic finger food, or as part of a summer mezze plate.

Preheat the oven to 180°C (350°F).

Wash the beetroot, wrap them individually in foil and place on a baking tray. Bake for 40 minutes, until a knife easily goes through the unwrapped beetroot. Unwrap the beetroot and allow to cool. Once they are cool enough to handle, peel the beetroot and cut them into 1 cm (½ inch) cubes. Put the beetroot in a large bowl.

Cut the salmon into cubes roughly the same size as the beetroot. Add the salmon, spring onion, horseradish, olive oil, lemon juice and coriander seeds to the beetroot and gently mix to combine. Season with freshly ground black pepper and garnish with baby beetroot leaves.

NOTE

The horseradish will be hot, so grate a quantity according to your liking.

400 g (14 oz) beetroot (beets)

300 g (10½ oz) salmon fillets, skin off and pin boned

65 g (2¼ oz/1 cup) chopped spring onions (scallions)

1 small horseradish, grated (see Note)

1½ tablespoons good-quality extra virgin olive oil

juice of 1 lemon

1 tablespoon coriander seeds, lightly toasted and coarsely crushed

baby beetroot leaves (beet greens), to garnish

FIG, HALOUMI AND FRESH ZA'ATAR LEAVES

SERVES 4 AS A STARTER

The combination of sweet and salty is intriguing and addictive. This salad is the Mediterranean equivalent of salted caramel in a savoury version and I can't get enough of it. It's very simple, quick and easy to make, but also elegant and impressive and a great starter when entertaining.

Heat the oil in a large frying pan over medium heat. Add the haloumi and cook for 2 minutes on each side, or until golden brown.

Remove any excess oil from the pan, leaving the haloumi in the pan, and add the honey. Increase the heat to high and allow the honey to reduce slightly. It will become sticky and glossy. Add the figs and cook until warmed through.

Arrange the haloumi and figs on a platter, scatter with the za'atar or oregano and the walnuts and spoon over the warm honey.

125 ml (4 fl oz/½ cup) light olive oil

500 g (1 lb 2 oz) haloumi cheese, cut into 8 slices

235 g (8½ oz/⅔ cup) honey

4 figs, halved lengthways

6 g (⅛ oz/½ cup) za'atar leaves or oregano leaves

100 g (3½ oz) walnuts, lightly toasted

QUINOA SALAD WITH NUTS AND POMEGRANATE

SERVES 6–8 AS A SIDE DISH

Although quinoa has been around for many years, it has only become popular in recent times. I like using a mixture of black, white and red quinoa as the colours look great. Combining the quinoa with nuts gives this salad a lovely texture.

Bring 375 ml (13 fl oz/1½ cups) water to the boil in a saucepan with a lid. Add the quinoa and reduce the heat to the lowest setting. Cover and cook for 15 minutes, then fluff up the quinoa grains with a fork. Allow the quinoa to cool.

Combine the nuts, pomegranate seeds, spring onion, parsley, oil and pomegranate molasses in a bowl, then add the cooled quinoa. Season with salt and freshly ground black pepper and gently mix together.

200 g (7 oz/1 cup) mixed quinoa

50 g (1¾ oz) pistachios, lightly toasted and crushed

50 g (1¾ oz) hazelnuts, lightly toasted and crushed

50 g (1¾ oz) natural almonds, lightly toasted and crushed

seeds of 1 pomegranate

5 spring onions (scallions), white part and part of the green part finely chopped

2 large handfuls flat-leaf (Italian) parsley, finely chopped

100 ml (3½ fl oz) olive oil

4 tablespoons pomegranate molasses

ROASTED BABY BEETROOT WITH LABNEH

SERVES 6

The creamy texture of the labneh and the earthy flavour of the beetroot work extraordinarily well together. You can use this dish any way you like—as a dip, salad or vegetable accompaniment.

Preheat the oven to 180°C (350°F).

Tear off several sheets of foil. Put 4–5 beetroot on one sheet of foil, add a sprig of thyme and drizzle with a tablespoon of olive oil. Wrap with another sheet of foil to enclose the beetroot. Repeat until all the beetroot are wrapped and you have 3 foil parcels. Place the beetroot parcels on a baking tray and roast for 35–40 minutes, until a knife easily goes through the unwrapped beetroot. Remove the beetroot from the oven but do not unwrap them; allow to cool for 10 minutes.

Once the beetroot are cool enough to handle, peel off the skin and cut into halves or quarters. Add to a bowl with the coriander seeds, thyme leaves, red wine vinegar and the 100 ml (3½ fl oz) of olive oil and mix to coat the beetroot. Season with salt and freshly ground black pepper. Set aside to marinate for 1 hour.

Spread the labneh over a large platter, top with the beetroot and sprinkle with the oregano leaves and crushed almonds. Season with salt and pepper and spoon the marinade over the top.

Pictured on page 70

12–15 baby beetroot (beets), trimmed and washed thoroughly

5 thyme sprigs, plus 2 teaspoons thyme leaves

100 ml (3½ fl oz) olive oil, plus extra for drizzling

1 tablespoon coriander seeds, lightly toasted and crushed

3 tablespoons red wine vinegar

350 g (12 oz) labneh

1 handful oregano, leaves picked

100 g (3½ oz) natural almonds, lightly toasted and coarsely crushed

BURRATA, RADISH AND CHIVE SALAD

SERVES 6 AS A SIDE DISH OR 2 AS A MAIN

I like to use a lot of different vegetables as bases for my salads—just not all at the same time. I choose one or two things that are beautiful at that moment, then pair them with other ingredients or spices that help to show them off. Here, peppery radishes balance the creaminess of the burrata cheese. It's a light summery dish that could easily be doubled or even tripled for a shared table and served with a warm crisp loaf of bread.

Blanch the sugar snap peas in a saucepan of boiling water, then drain and plunge them into a bowl of iced water to cool.

Tear the burrata into a large serving bowl—the cream will ooze out into the bowl and form part of the dressing. Spread the burrata around the bowl. Scatter half the sugar snap peas over the burrata. Season with sea salt, half the olive oil and half the lemon juice. Add the radishes, the remaining sugar snap peas and the chives.

Drizzle the remaining oil and lemon juice over the salad and season with sea salt and cracked black pepper.

NOTE

This salad is made in the bowl that you are going to serve it in. I suggest using a large, flat salad bowl with a rim.

150 g (5½ oz) sugar snap peas, trimmed

3 x 100 g (3½ oz) burrata cheese balls, drained

sea salt

4 tablespoons extra virgin olive oil

juice of 2 lemons

100 g (3½ oz/1 bunch) small radishes, very thinly sliced

30 g (1 oz) chives, cut into 3 cm (1¼ inch) lengths

KRISTY'S FAVOURITE EGGPLANT SALAD

SERVES 6–8 AS A SIDE DISH

I first made this salad for Kristy and her family many years ago and they loved it. It was their introduction to using a lot of nuts and herbs in a salad and the fried eggplant was something they had never really tried. The salad became the most requested dish at family functions, so much so that the recipe appeared in a family cookbook that Kristy and her cousin put together. The whole family now embraces the idea of nuts and herbs in salads.

Heat the vegetable oil in a large, deep frying pan over medium heat. Fry the eggplant in batches for 8–10 minutes each batch, until golden brown. Drain on paper towel and set aside.

Once all the eggplant has been cooked, add the almonds to the oil and cook for 3–5 minutes, until light golden (they will continue to cook after you take them out of the oil). Drain the almonds on paper towel.

Add the pine nuts to the oil and cook for 2 minutes, or until light golden. Use a slotted spoon to remove the pine nuts from the oil and drain on paper towel.

Put the tomato, spring onion, onion, coriander and lemon juice in a large bowl and mix until well combined. Add the eggplant, almonds and pine nuts. Season with salt and freshly ground black pepper and serve drizzled with the olive oil.

NOTE

It might sound like there is a lot of vegetable oil used to fry the eggplant, but this amount will allow the eggplant to cook faster and it will actually absorb less oil when frying.

1 litre (35 fl oz/4 cups) vegetable oil, for frying

2 eggplants (aubergines), peeled and cut into 2 cm (¾ inch) cubes

200 g (7 oz/1¼ cups) natural almonds

4 tablespoons pine nuts

2 tomatoes, chopped

5 spring onions (scallions), white and part of the green finely chopped

½ red onion, finely chopped

1 large handful coriander (cilantro), chopped

juice of 2 lemons

3 teaspoons good-quality extra virgin olive oil

ORANGE, HARISSA AND BLACK OLIVE SALAD

SERVES 4–6 AS A SIDE DISH

This salad is part of a sashimi dish that has been on the Kepos & Co. menu. It works really well as part of a shared table if you are serving fish dishes. Surprisingly, all the ingredients do work well together—the saltiness of the olives balances the sweetness of the oranges, and the harissa adds a lovely complexity to it.

Arrange the orange segments and olives on a platter. Scatter the coriander leaves over the top.

Mix the harissa with the olive oil, then drizzle it over the salad.

6 oranges, peeled and segmented (page 245)

50 g (1¾ oz) pitted black olives, halved

1 small handful coriander (cilantro), leaves picked

4 tablespoons harissa (page 220)

4 tablespoons olive oil

FREEKEH, CORIANDER AND ALMOND SALAD

SERVES 6 AS A SIDE DISH OR 4 AS A MAIN

Eating freekeh always makes me feel healthy. The thing I love about this salad is that, while it's an excellent companion to a meat, fish or chicken dish, it's just as delicious on its own. Transform it into a suitable dish for your vegan friends by leaving out the cheese.

Put the freekeh in a large saucepan with plenty of water. Bring to the boil over high heat, then reduce the heat to medium–low and cook for 25–30 minutes, until the freekeh is tender but does not break apart.

Coarsely chop half the coriander and put it in a food processor. Add the garlic and blitz for 30 seconds. Add the grated cheese and almond meal and blend for 2 minutes, or until the mixture forms a paste. Add the olive oil, lemon zest and lemon juice and season with salt. Blend until combined—the mixture should look like pesto and have a similar consistency. Set aside.

Heat the barbecue or chargrill pan to medium–high. Rub the asparagus spears with a little olive oil and then grill until done to your liking—I like quite a bit of colour on my asparagus. Set aside to cool and then cut the asparagus spears into thirds.

Put the cooked freekeh in a large serving bowl. Pick the leaves from the remaining coriander and add them to the bowl along with the coriander paste, crushed almonds and asparagus. Toss to combine and season with additional salt if needed.

250 g (9 oz/1 cup) freekeh

2 large handfuls coriander (cilantro)

2 garlic cloves

2 tablespoons grated haloumi or parmesan cheese

2 tablespoons almond meal

3 tablespoons olive oil, plus extra for cooking

grated zest and juice of ½ lemon

2 bunches asparagus, peeled and trimmed

150 g (5½ oz) natural almonds, lightly toasted and coarsely crushed

GREEK SALAD

SERVES 6–8 AS A SIDE DISH OR 4 AS A MAIN

Greek salad is a classic that can be served with any meal or as a meal on its own. Last time I went home it was served everywhere. This recipe is a modernised version of the classic.

Put the tomatoes, cucumbers, onion, olives, chillies and oregano in a bowl and gently mix to combine. Pour in the lemon juice and half the oil and season with freshly ground black pepper.

Spoon the salad onto a platter and top with the feta. Drizzle with the remaining oil and garnish with the salt.

NOTES

I prefer soft Danish feta cheese but any other feta is also suitable.

Pictured on page 23

500 g (1 lb 2 oz) mixed heirloom tomatoes, coarsely chopped

2 Lebanese (short) cucumbers, coarsely chopped

½ red onion, thinly sliced

50 g (1¾ oz) pitted black olives

40 g (1½ oz) pickled Middle Eastern or jalapeño chillies

3 tablespoons oregano leaves

juice of 1 lemon

100 ml (3½ fl oz) olive oil

300 g (10½ oz) feta cheese, cut into large cubes

black volcanic salt or sea salt flakes, to garnish

TZATZIKI SALAD

SERVES 6–8 AS A SIDE DISH

I've taken a recipe that's normally a dip and turned it into a salad. It's a lovely refreshing dish that works well with roasted lamb. You could toss some shredded chicken or fish through the salad for a main meal.

Cut the cucumbers in half lengthways. Scoop out and discard some of the seeds. Cut the cucumbers into batons.

Put the cucumber in a large bowl with the chilli, mint and watercress, and mix with your hands to combine.

To make the dressing, put the yoghurt, garlic, mint and oil in a bowl and mix together. Season with salt and freshly ground black pepper.

Toss the dressing through the salad. Taste and add extra seasoning if needed.

Pictured on page 71

5 Lebanese (short) cucumbers
1 large fresh green chilli, sliced
1 large handful mint leaves, roughly torn
1 bunch watercress, leaves picked

DRESSING
250 g (9 oz) Greek-style yoghurt
1 garlic clove, crushed
2 teaspoons dried mint
50 ml (1½ fl oz) olive oil

1. **ZUCCHINI AND ZA'ATAR EMPANADA** see page 41
2. **ROASTED BABY BEETROOT WITH LABNEH** see page 59
3. **WHITE BEAN AND SUMAC SALAD** see page 52
4. **TZATZIKI SALAD** see page 69

GRILLED CHILLI, GARLIC AND CORIANDER SALAD

SERVES 6 AS A SIDE DISH

If you like things spicy, this salad makes a great addition to a shared table. Grilling the chillies tones down their heat and even brings out a little sweetness. You could also serve this as a salsa with a piece of steak. The leftovers are fantastic on sandwiches.

Heat the barbecue to high. Drizzle the fresh chillies with vegetable oil, then cook, turning, until scorched all over. Transfer to a bowl, cover with plastic wrap and set aside until the chillies come to room temperature. Peel the skin off the chillies, leaving the chillies whole.

Transfer the chillies to a serving bowl and mix in the garlic, coriander, pickled chillies, olive oil and vinegar. Season with the sea salt flakes and some freshly ground black pepper.

NOTE

This dish is best served at room temperature.

Pictured on page 99

300 g (10½ oz) mixed large fresh red and green chillies

vegetable oil, for drizzling

2 garlic cloves, thinly sliced

1 large handful coriander (cilantro), coarsely chopped

50 g (1¾ oz) pickled Middle Eastern or jalapeño chillies

100 ml (3½ fl oz) olive oil

3 tablespoons red wine vinegar

sea salt flakes, to taste

POTATO, WHITE ANCHOVY AND CAPER SALAD

SERVES 6

There are so many different versions of potato salad. I prefer the ones that don't have a mayonnaise-based dressing. This version is light and zingy and can work well on its own or with a piece of fish. It's an easy dish to have in your repertoire as you can prepare it ahead of time when you have guests coming over.

Fill a large saucepan with water and add the potatoes. Bring to the boil and cook over medium heat for 25–30 minutes, until the potatoes are cooked through but still firm. Drain and set aside to cool.

Peel the cooled potatoes and add them to a large bowl along with the remaining ingredients. Gently mix to combine.

600 g (1 lb 5 oz) kipfler (fingerling) potatoes

1 small red onion, thinly sliced

150 g (5½ oz) white anchovy fillets in oil, drained

50 g (1¾ oz) caperberries in vinegar, drained

1 small handful dill

3 tablespoons sesame seeds, toasted

1 tablespoon fennel seeds, lightly toasted and crushed

grated zest and juice of 1 lemon

125 ml (4 fl oz/½ cup) olive oil

HEIRLOOM CARROT SALAD

SERVES 6–8 AS A SIDE DISH

Carrots are such a versatile vegetable. They are prepared in three different ways in this salad, giving three different textures and transforming the humble carrot into a very noble dish.

Blanch a third of the heirloom carrots in boiling water for 2–3 minutes. Drain and then refresh in cold water. Cut another third of the carrots into large chunks. Peel the remaining carrots into ribbons.

Mix all the carrots, the nuts, cumin seeds, ground cumin, oil, vinegar and parsley in a large bowl. Toss lightly and season with salt and freshly cracked black pepper to taste.

Scatter half the goat's cheese into a serving bowl. Add the carrot mixture and then top with the remaining goat's cheese and a few small coriander leaves, if you like.

300 g (10½ oz/2 bunches) heirloom carrots, trimmed

1 carrot, peeled and cut into large chunks

100 g (3½ oz) hazelnuts, toasted, skinned and coarsely chopped

4 tablespoons pine nuts, lightly toasted

1 tablespoon cumin seeds, toasted and lightly crushed

½ teaspoon ground cumin

50 ml (1½ fl oz) olive oil

1½ tablespoons red wine vinegar

1 large handful flat-leaf (Italian) parsley, finely chopped

100 g (3½ oz) goat's cheese

micro coriander leaves, for garnish (optional)

KOHLRABI AND FENNEL SALAD

SERVES 6–8 AS A SIDE DISH

As much as I love mayonnaise, I find there are too many salad recipes with a mayonnaise-based dressing. I like to use yoghurt as it makes the dish much lighter and healthier.

Trim the base of the kohlrabi, then cut it into thin discs, about 5 mm (¼ inch) thick. Cut the discs into julienne strips and place in a bowl of cold water.

Cut off the fennel fronds and discard, and trim the base. Using a mandolin, shave the fennel bulb into thin slices. Add to the water with the kohlrabi.

Drain the kohlrabi and fennel well. Transfer to a large bowl, add the remaining ingredients and season with salt and freshly ground black pepper. Mix to combine.

1 large or 2 small kohlrabi bulbs

1 large fennel bulb

1 handful dill, leaves picked and coarsely chopped

1 large handful flat-leaf (Italian) parsley, coarsely chopped

150 g (5½ oz) Greek-style yoghurt

juice of ½ lemon

1½ tablespoons olive oil

PUY LENTIL AND TOMATO SALAD

SERVES 6–8 AS A SIDE DISH

The older I get, the more I enjoy lentils, grains and other legumes. This is a very simple salad but it's certainly very filling and makes you feel like you've eaten something healthy. It's a great option when you have vegan friends over for a meal.

Put the lentils in a large saucepan with plenty of water over high heat. Bring to the boil and cook for 15 minutes, or until the lentils are tender but not breaking apart. Drain and refresh in cold water so the lentils do not continue to cook.

Place the lentils in a large bowl and gently mix with the rest of the ingredients. Serve on a platter.

200 g (7 oz) puy lentils or tiny blue-green lentils

2 small fresh green chillies, finely chopped

300 g (10½ oz) heirloom cherry tomatoes, halved

1 large handful mint, finely chopped

1 large handful flat-leaf (Italian) parsley, finely chopped

3 French shallots, finely chopped

50 ml (1½ fl oz) olive oil

grated zest and juice of 1 lemon

SOURDOUGH FATTOUSH SALAD

SERVES 6–8 AS A SIDE DISH

We always struggle to use up stale bread at home, so this recipe is great to make when you don't manage to eat the whole loaf. Traditionally it's made with crispy flatbread, but I find we use more sourdough than flatbread so I've adjusted the recipe to reflect what most people have at home.

Preheat the oven to 170°C (340°F).

Put the bread cubes on a baking tray, drizzle with the oil and toss to combine. Bake for about 7–8 minutes, until the bread is toasted and golden. Set aside to cool.

To make the dressing, mix all the ingredients together and season with salt and freshly ground black pepper.

Put the bread cubes, cucumber, tomato, onion and herbs in a large bowl and mix to combine. Pour the dressing over and lightly toss with your hands. Drizzle the pomegranate molasses over the top.

¼ loaf sourdough bread, cut into large cubes

100 ml (3½ fl oz) olive oil

2 small Lebanese (short) cucumbers, coarsely chopped

2 vine-ripened tomatoes, coarsely chopped

½ small red onion, cut into thin wedges

3 tablespoons oregano leaves

1 handful coriander (cilantro) leaves

2 tablespoons pomegranate molasses

DRESSING

3 tablespoons olive oil

3 tablespoons lemon juice

3 garlic cloves, crushed

1 tablespoon sumac

TUNISIAN TUNA SALAD

SERVES 4

The 'sabich' or 'sabih' is a classic Middle Eastern sandwich that happens to have all the textures needed for a delicious salad. It has become one of my favourite salads to make because it doesn't require too much effort, as everything can be prepared in advance. Although you can use tinned tuna, if you have the time I suggest preserving your own tuna as it isn't difficult and the results are very rewarding.

Cook the potatoes in a large saucepan of boiling water until tender. Drain and cool, then peel and cut into chunks.

Combine the potato chunks, olives, tomato, cucumber and coriander in a large bowl and mix together.

To make the dressing, combine the harissa, oil and vinegar in a bowl. Season with salt and freshly ground black pepper and mix together until combined.

Carefully break open the eggs and arrange them on top of the salad. Break the tuna into pieces and add it to the salad. Drizzle the dressing over the top, season with black pepper and serve garnished with a few sprigs of coriander.

200 g (7 oz) kipfler (fingerling) potatoes

50 g (1¾ oz) pitted black olives

2 tomatoes, cut into wedges

1 Lebanese (short) cucumber, chopped

3 tablespoons coarsely chopped coriander (cilantro), plus a few sprigs for garnish

3 soft-boiled eggs

250 g (9 oz) preserved tuna (page 234) or tinned tuna

DRESSING

2 tablespoons harissa

3 tablespoons olive oil

3 tablespoons red wine vinegar

CHAPTER THREE

MAINS

Growing up in Israel, my mum would prepare several dishes for our main meal of the day and these would all become part of our sharing table. It was very different to the individually plated meal of meat and three veg that Kristy's family ate each night. There are recipes in this chapter that can be prepared quickly, such as Barbecued prawns with chermoula, which only takes a few minutes to cook. If you have more time on your hands, you should try the Lamb kanafeh or the cabbage leaves stuffed with rice and veal—both of those represent true comfort food.

ROAST CHICKEN WITH SOURDOUGH STUFFING

SERVES 4–6

I've added Middle Eastern flavours to create my take on the classic chicken with bread stuffing. It's a great Sunday roast and the stuffing is so good it could be a meal on its own.

Preheat the oven to 190°C (375°F).

To make the stuffing, heat the oil in a frying pan over medium heat. Cook the onion and garlic until golden brown. Remove from the heat and set aside.

Rinse the bread under cold water for a few seconds to dampen it, then squeeze out the excess water. Put the bread in a large bowl with the beef, pistachios, pine nuts, cinnamon and onion mixture. Season with salt and freshly ground black pepper.

Rinse the chicken, then pat dry with paper towel. Stuff the cavity of the chicken with the sourdough stuffing.

Put the oil, butter and parsley in a bowl and mix until combined. Carefully rub the mixture between the chicken skin and flesh.

Put the chicken in a roasting tin and bake for 40–45 minutes, until golden and cooked through.

Pictured on page 129

1 large free-range chicken, around 1.5–2 kg (3 lb 5 oz–4 lb 8 oz)
100 ml (3½ fl oz) olive oil
100 g (3½ oz) butter, at room temperature
1 handful flat-leaf (Italian) parsley, leaves chopped

STUFFING

3 tablespoons olive oil
1 large brown onion, chopped
3 garlic cloves, finely chopped
¼ loaf sourdough bread, crusts removed
200 g (7 oz) minced (ground) beef
100 g (3½ oz/⅔ cup) pistachios, lightly toasted
100 g (3½ oz/⅔ cup) pine nuts, lightly toasted
1 tablespoon ground cinnamon

PERSIAN CRANBERRY RICE PILAF

SERVES 8 AS A SIDE DISH

When I was young, my mum wouldn't usually cook rice dishes when guests came over for dinner because she thought they weren't sophisticated enough. I have to disagree with my mum regarding this fragrant saffron rice with nuts and cranberries. It can be a winning side dish, and is lovely with braised meat. I am a big fan of adding nuts to savoury dishes as they provide an added texture and beautiful flavour.

Put the ghee in a large saucepan with a lid and place over medium heat. Add the rice and cook, stirring, for 1 minute. Add the turmeric, salt and sugar and stir for 1 minute, or until the rice is toasted. Pour in the boiling water or stock and add the saffron threads and soaking water. Bring to the boil, then cover the pan, reduce the heat to low and cook for 18 minutes.

Remove the saucepan from the heat and leave the pilaf to rest for 5–10 minutes, keeping the lid on.

Using a fork, fluff up the rice and fold in the cranberries or barberries, pistachios, chives and extra ghee.

3 tablespoons ghee, plus 3 tablespoons extra, to serve

400 g (14 oz/2 cups) basmati rice

½ teaspoon ground turmeric

1 teaspoon salt

2 teaspoons sugar

750 ml (26 fl oz/3 cups) boiling water or vegetable stock

pinch of saffron threads, soaked in 2 tablespoons warm water

145 g (5 oz/1 cup) cranberries or barberries

60 g (2¼ oz) pistachios, coarsely crushed

2 bunches chives, finely chopped

1. **SILVERBEET WITH HARISSA** see page 127
2. **COUSCOUS WITH NUTS AND ROSE PETALS** see page 91
3. **ASPARAGUS, BLACK OLIVES AND TOMATOES** see page 126
4. **FISH AND CHICKPEA STEW** see page 90

FISH AND CHICKPEA STEW

SERVES 6

For an effortless dinner that's full of flavour, you can't really beat this fish stew. It's a simplified version of a fish tagine that you can cook when you don't want the house to smell like fish. It's great served with couscous or rice to soak up the delicious sauce.

Heat the olive oil in a large frying pan with a lid over medium heat. Sauté the onion and garlic until transparent. Add the turmeric and cumin and cook for 1 minute. Add the saffron and stock and bring to the boil. Reduce the heat to medium–low, add the chickpeas and cook for 10 minutes.

Add the fish pieces, sprinkle with the chilli flakes and season with salt and freshly ground black pepper. Cover the pan and cook over low heat for 5 minutes. Carefully turn the fish pieces over, cover and cook for 8–10 minutes, until the fish is done to your liking.

Serve the stew garnished with the chopped coriander.

Pictured on page 89

4 tablespoons olive oil

1 large brown onion, chopped

2 garlic cloves

3 teaspoons ground turmeric

1 teaspoon ground cumin

pinch of saffron threads

500 ml (17 fl oz/2 cups) fish or vegetable stock

400 g (14 oz) cooked or tinned chickpeas

1 kg (2 lb 4 oz) firm white fish fillets, such as blue-eye trevalla, skin off and cut into large chunks

1 teaspoon chilli flakes

1 large handful coriander (cilantro), coarsely chopped

COUSCOUS WITH NUTS AND ROSE PETALS

SERVES 4–6

Couscous is a versatile ingredient that can adapt itself to many different dishes and flavours. I like the nuts in this version, and it goes well with a piece of fish or meat that has juices that can soak into the couscous.

Put the couscous in a heatproof bowl with the salt and 2 tablespoons of the olive oil. Mix together, rubbing the couscous with your fingers to help it absorb the oil. Pour in the boiling water and tightly cover the bowl with plastic wrap. Set aside in a warm place for 12–15 minutes. Lightly fluff the couscous with a fork, without overworking it. Set aside to cool to room temperature.

Add the remaining oil and the rest of the ingredients—except the pomegranate seeds—to the couscous and mix together. Check for seasoning—you may need to add more salt and some freshly ground black pepper. Tap a few pomegranate seeds over the couscous just before serving, if you like.

Pictured on page 88

150 g (5½ oz) couscous

1 tablespoon salt

100 ml (3½ fl oz) olive oil

150 ml (5 fl oz) boiling water

100 g (3½ oz/⅔ cup) pine nuts, lightly toasted

4 tablespoons pistachios, lightly toasted and coarsely chopped

30 g (1 oz/1 cup) chopped flat-leaf (Italian) parsley

grated zest of 1 lemon

2 tablespoons dried mint

3 tablespoons good-quality white wine vinegar

2 tablespoons edible dried rose petals

seeds of ½ pomegranate (optional)

MOROCCAN LAMB AND PINE NUT CIGARS

MAKES 10

I like serving these rolls for breakfast or brunch on the weekend alongside poached eggs and a watercress salad for a nice peppery flavour. They are also good as a nibble with drinks and you can make them smaller to serve with canapés.

Heat the olive oil in a frying pan over medium heat. Sauté the onion for 3–5 minutes, until golden. Increase the heat to high and add the lamb. Cook, breaking up the lumps with a spoon and stirring, for 5 minutes. Stir in the chermoula and cook for 1 minute. (The lamb doesn't need to be cooked through at this point as it will cook further when you fry the rolls.) Stir in the pine nuts then set aside to cool to room temperature.

Divide the lamb mixture into 10 portions. Lay a spring roll wrapper on a board and brush one edge with the beaten egg. Place a portion of the lamb mixture on the opposite edge. Fold in the sides and roll up into a cigar shape. Seal the edges with more egg. Repeat with the remaining wrappers and lamb mixture.

Put the vegetable oil in a deep-fryer or a large, deep saucepan and heat to 170°C (340°F). If you don't have a thermometer, drop in a cube of bread—the oil is hot enough when the bread turns golden brown in 20 seconds. Lower the cigars into the hot oil and cook in batches for 2–3 minutes, until golden and crisp. Remove and drain on paper towel. Serve hot.

3 tablespoons olive oil

1 brown onion, finely chopped

600 g (1 lb 5 oz) minced (ground) lamb

3 tablespoons chermoula (page 225)

4 tablespoons pine nuts

10 x 20 cm (8 inch) square spring roll wrappers

1 egg, lightly beaten

vegetable oil, for deep-frying

PUMPKIN KIBBEH WITH MOZZARELLA

SERVES 6–8 AS A MAIN OR 8–10 AS A SIDE DISH

I sometimes find it hard to come up with a hearty vegetarian main course that isn't a risotto or pasta. This is a perfect vegetarian dish that even meat eaters will love. It's a take on the traditional kibbeh that is made with minced (ground) meat and burghul (bulgur). Here, I have substituted pumpkin for the meat and added cheese for the middle layer.

Preheat the oven to 180°C (350°F). Line a baking tray with baking paper.

Toss the pumpkin with the oil, salt and peeled garlic cloves and spread over the baking tray. Bake for about 20 minutes, or until the pumpkin is soft. If the pumpkin is browning too quickly, reduce the temperature. Remove from the oven and set aside, but leave the oven turned on.

Meanwhile, put the burghul in a large heatproof bowl and pour in the boiling water. Soak the burghul for about 6 minutes, then drain. During this time the burghul will soak up a lot of the water. Once cool enough to handle, squeeze out any excess water.

Transfer the roasted pumpkin to a large bowl and mash with a potato masher or a fork, then mix in the burghul. Add the ground cinnamon and cumin and season with salt and freshly ground black pepper. Mix to combine.

Lightly brush a 20 x 30 cm (8 x 12 inch) rectangular ovenproof dish or roasting tin with olive oil and line the base with baking paper. Spread half the pumpkin and burghul mixture over the base of the dish. Add the grated mozzarella cheese, then top with the remaining pumpkin mixture and smooth the top with the back of a spoon. Using a sharp knife, score the top into diamonds.

Bake the pumpkin kibbeh for 25 minutes, or longer if you prefer a very crisp topping.

800 g–1 kg (1 lb 12 oz–2 lb 4 oz) chopped, peeled kent pumpkin

3 tablespoons olive oil, plus extra for brushing

1 tablespoon salt

2 garlic cloves

200 g (7 oz) coarse burghul (bulgur)

1.5 litres (52 fl oz/6 cups) boiling water

¼ teaspoon ground cinnamon

½ teaspoon ground cumin

400 g (14 oz) mozzarella cheese, grated

LAMB KANAFEH

SERVES 6–8

Kataifi pastry is frequently used in Middle Eastern sweets. Here, the crisp pastry sits on top of a braised lamb base. It's a great dish to make ahead of time—add the kataifi and cook it just before serving so that it stays crisp.

Heat the oil in a large saucepan over medium heat. Sear the lamb in batches until golden brown. Remove from the pan and set aside.

Add the onion, chilli and garlic to the pan and sauté for 4–5 minutes, until transparent. Add the spices and fry for 1 minute. Pour in the wine and cook for 3–4 minutes, until the liquid has reduced by half. Return the lamb to the saucepan along with the chopped tomatoes and stock. Bring to the boil, then reduce the heat to medium-low and cook for about 3 hours, stirring occasionally.

Stir in the tomato paste and cook for a further 20 minutes, or until the sauce has reduced and thickened. Stir in the coriander and set aside.

Preheat the oven to 180°C (350°F).

Separate the kataifi pastry by shredding it in a large bowl. Pour in the melted butter and mix with your hands to combine.

Pour the lamb into a 25 cm (10 inch) square ovenproof dish or a 35 cm (14 inch) round ovenproof dish. Top with the shredded kataifi. Bake for 20–25 minutes, until the kataifi is golden. Remove from the oven and serve dolloped with the yoghurt.

Also pictured on page 99

4 tablespoons olive oil

1 kg (2 lb 4 oz) lamb shoulder, cut into 4 cm (1½ inch) cubes

2 small brown onions, chopped

2 small fresh green chillies, chopped

4 garlic cloves, chopped

pinch of saffron threads

2 tablespoons sweet paprika

1 tablespoon ground cumin

100 ml (3½ fl oz) white wine

2 x 400 g (14 oz) tins chopped tomatoes or 800 g (1 lb 12 oz) fresh tomatoes, chopped

1.5 litres (52 fl oz/6 cups) chicken stock

4 tablespoons tomato paste (concentrated purée)

1 large handful coriander (cilantro), leaves picked and coarsely chopped

200 g (7 oz) kataifi pastry

20 g (¾ oz) butter, melted

4 tablespoons Greek-style yoghurt

BARBECUED PRAWNS WITH CHERMOULA

SERVES 4–6

As a chef, I've noticed that friends are reluctant to invite me over for a meal. Perhaps they think they need to cook something fancy or complicated to impress me, but that's not the case. One night, Kristy and I were invited to a friend's house for dinner where we were served fresh cooked prawns, soft white rolls and a good-quality mayonnaise. We were in food heaven! The simple things in life tend to be the best, and this is definitely true of food. These prawns prove you don't need to slave over a stove to impress. They're great as a fancy finger food or can be served with other dishes as a main meal.

Heat the barbecue or a chargrill pan to high.

Put the prawns in a large bowl. Add the chermoula and olive oil and mix to combine.

Cook the prawns in batches on the hot barbecue or chargrill pan for 1 minute on each side, or until done to your liking.

Arrange the cooked prawns on a platter. Drizzle with olive oil, season with salt and freshly ground black pepper and scatter with the basil.

1 kg (2 lb 4 oz) raw large prawns (shrimp), about 20–25 prawns

5 tablespoons chermoula (page 225)

3 tablespoons olive oil, plus extra for drizzling

20 basil leaves, coarsely chopped

SWEET AND SOUR STUFFED ONIONS

SERVES 6–8

Not many people think of Middle Eastern food as salty, sour and sweet, as that combination is usually associated with Asian cuisine. This dish is an interesting use of onions and unusual Middle Eastern flavours. It takes a bit of time to prepare but is definitely worth the effort.

Peel the onions and cut them in half lengthways. Put them in a large saucepan of boiling water, then reduce the heat and simmer for 10–15 minutes, until tender. Drain and set aside to cool. When the onions are cool enough to handle, separate the layers.

Meanwhile, soak the raisins in hot water for 5 minutes, then drain.

Combine the beef, rice, raisins, spices and oil in a bowl and season with salt and freshly ground black pepper.

Stuff each onion layer with some of the beef mixture and press firmly. Arrange in a large flameproof casserole dish in a single layer with the opening on the bottom.

Combine the tamarind paste, lemon juice and stock and season with salt. Pour the mixture over the onions. Bring to the boil over medium heat, then cover, reduce the heat to low and cook for 40 minutes. Remove the lid and cook for a further 5 minutes.

3 large red or brown onions

50 g (1¾ oz) raisins

350 g (12 oz) coarsely minced (ground) beef

100 g (3½ oz/½ cup) long-grain rice

½ teaspoon ground cinnamon

½ teaspoon ground cumin

½ teaspoon ground allspice

4 tablespoons olive oil

3 tablespoons tamarind paste

juice of 1 lemon

500 ml (17 fl oz/2 cups) vegetable or chicken stock

CABBAGE LEAVES STUFFED WITH RICE AND VEAL

SERVES 8–10

My mother and aunties used to make trays of these stuffed leaves when I was young, and back then, the smell of cabbage through the house was not my favourite thing. I suppose these are probably my version of brussels sprouts, which many people seem to grow up disliking for similar reasons. As an adult, I've developed a real appreciation for this dish and can't believe I rebelled against eating it for so many years. I now find it comforting and delicious. The leaves stay more al dente than other stuffed vegetables, and the meat is used sparingly, almost as a seasoning through the rice. The garlic gets sweet and tender as it cooks, and sucking it out of the clove is one of my favourite things. Once these are cooked they don't require much. A squeeze of lemon and I'm happy.

Fill a saucepan that is large enough to hold the whole cabbage to three-quarters full with water. Bring to the boil, then add the cabbage and cook for 10 minutes.

Drain and cool the cabbage under running water. Once cool, cut off the core and then carefully release the leaves, setting any broken ones aside. If necessary, trim the leaves so that they are roughly the same size.

Put the rice in a bowl and wash thoroughly, then discard the water and repeat. Add the veal, pine nuts, mint and olive oil and season with salt and freshly ground black pepper. Gently mix until just combined, without breaking up the rice.

Place 2½ tablespoons of the mixture on each cabbage leaf, fold in the sides and roll into a cigar shape.

Put all the broken cabbage leaves in a large saucepan to form a base. Gently lay the rolled cabbage leaves on top, packing them in tightly. Add the fennel seeds and unpeeled garlic cloves, pour in the chicken stock and season with salt and pepper. Lay a sheet of baking paper on top of the rolls and place a heatproof plate on top. Bring to the boil over medium heat, then reduce the heat to low and cook for 35–40 minutes, until cooked through.

1 large whole cabbage

400 g (14 oz/2 cups) long-grain rice

500 g (1 lb 2 oz) coarsely minced (ground) veal

100 g (3½ oz/⅔ cup) pine nuts, lightly toasted

2 tablespoons dried mint

100 ml (3½ fl oz) olive oil

1 tablespoon fennel seeds

1 garlic bulb, cloves separated

2 litres (70 fl oz/8 cups) chicken stock

MOUSSAKA

SERVES 8–10

The easiest way to introduce this dish is by describing it as
the Greek version of lasagne. It's a great dish to serve a crowd,
and works well as part of a shared table or on its own with
a leafy salad.

Preheat the oven to 180°C (350°F). Line 2 large baking trays with
baking paper.

Trim the bases and stalks off the eggplants and cut them lengthways
into 1 cm (½ inch) thick pieces. Lay the eggplant slices on the trays
and drizzle with olive oil. Bake for 20 minutes, then turn and cook
for another 10 minutes. The eggplants will have some colour and be
cooked through but still firm. Set aside until you are assembling the
moussaka, but leave the oven turned on.

Heat the olive oil in a large frying pan over medium heat. Cook the
onion for 3–5 minutes, until golden. Add the lamb and cook for
5 minutes, stirring and breaking it up. Drain off any fat. Add the
chopped tomatoes, tomato passata or water, tomato paste, cinnamon
and dried oregano. Season with salt and freshly ground black pepper.
Reduce the heat to medium-low and simmer for 20–25 minutes, until
the sauce has thickened and reduced slightly. Taste and add extra
seasoning if needed.

While the lamb is cooking, make the béchamel sauce. Melt the butter
in a saucepan over medium heat. Add the flour and stir for 1 minute.
Slowly add the warm milk, stirring to make a smooth sauce. Cook for
5 minutes, or until the sauce has thickened.

Combine the breadcrumbs with the fresh oregano and season with
salt and freshly ground black pepper.

Layer half the roasted eggplant slices in the base of a lightly greased
20 x 30 cm (8 x 12 inch) ovenproof dish, then top with half the lamb
mixture and half the béchamel sauce. Sprinkle half the breadcrumbs
and oregano over the sauce. Repeat with the remaining eggplant, lamb
mixture, sauce and breadcrumb mixture. Bake for 40–45 minutes, until
the top is golden. Let the moussaka rest for 10 minutes before slicing
and serving.

3 large eggplants (aubergines)

2 tablespoons olive oil, plus extra for drizzling

1 brown onion, finely chopped

600 g (1 lb 5 oz) minced (ground) lamb

400 g (14 oz) tin chopped tomatoes

250 ml (9 fl oz/1 cup) tomato passata (puréed
tomatoes) or water

2 tablespoons tomato paste (concentrated purée)

½ teaspoon ground cinnamon

1 teaspoon dried oregano

50 g (1¾ oz) dry breadcrumbs

1 oregano sprig, leaves picked and finely chopped

BÉCHAMEL SAUCE

75 g (2½ oz) butter

75 g (2½ oz/½ cup) plain (all-purpose) flour

750 ml (26 fl oz/3 cups) milk, warmed

GREEN LENTIL, TOMATO AND KALE SOUP

SERVES 6–8

I'm not a big fan of puréed soup, or what I call 'mushy soup', as I like to experience the different textures of the ingredients. This chunky soup is quick and easy to make, and I love the combination of the green lentils and kale.

Heat the oil in a very large saucepan over medium heat. Add the onion, garlic and celery and sweat for 3–5 minutes. Add the tomato paste and cook for 1 minute. Stir in the tomato and cook for another minute, then pour in the stock.

Put the lentils in a fine sieve and rinse well under running water. Add to the pan and cook for 25–30 minutes, until the lentils are soft and just holding together. You will need to skim the surface occasionally but try not to take out too many lentils.

Season the soup with salt and freshly ground black pepper, then add the kale, pushing it down into the soup. Cook until the kale is wilted, about 2–3 minutes.

Ladle the soup into bowls and serve with a drizzle of good-quality olive oil.

4 tablespoons olive oil, plus extra to serve

1 brown onion, finely chopped

3 garlic cloves, finely chopped

2 celery stalks with leaves, finely chopped

2 tablespoons tomato paste (concentrated purée)

4 ripe tomatoes, diced

2.5 litres (87 fl oz/10 cups) chicken stock

200 g (7 oz) green lentils

1 small bunch kale, stalks removed, coarsely chopped

STUFFED QUAILS WITH SPICY SAUSAGE, PINE NUTS AND DATES

SERVES 6

My favourite thing about these birds is the combination of flavours: sweetness from the dates, and salty and spicy flavours from the sujuk, a spicy Armenian sausage. It's not a classic Middle Eastern combination but it creates a magical flavour. Stuffing and cooking game birds takes me back to childhood and reminds me of my Nana. She was known for her adventurous cooking style and patience with fiddly preparation. She would regularly pester the local butcher for the best cuts of meat and the two of them would have a playful argument that would cause her to leave. He'd chase after her and eventually she'd come back and buy the meat

Preheat the oven to 190°C (375°F).

To make the stuffing, heat a frying pan over medium heat and fry the chorizo until crisp. Add the onion and sauté for 3–5 minutes, until golden. Transfer the chorizo and onion to a bowl and set aside to cool. Add the pine nuts, dates and mint, season with salt and freshly ground black pepper and mix to combine.

Divide the stuffing into 6 portions and use it to stuff the butterflied quails. Close the quails and secure them with strong toothpicks to hold the stuffing in place.

Heat the olive oil in a frying pan over medium heat. Sear the quails until golden brown, then transfer to a baking tray and bake for 5–6 minutes. Remove from the oven, brush with the date molasses and rest for 3 minutes before serving.

NOTE

You can sear the quails in an ovenproof frying pan, then transfer the pan directly to the oven to bake the quails.

6 quails, butterflied
2 tablespoons olive oil
160 ml (5¼ fl oz) date molasses

STUFFING

300 g (10½ oz) sujuk or chorizo sausage, chopped
½ brown onion, chopped
160 g (5½ oz) pine nuts, toasted
150 g (5½ oz) dried dates, pitted and chopped
1 handful mint leaves, chopped

SPINACH AND VEAL MEATBALLS

SERVES 4

You can never have enough meatball recipes in your repertoire. This is a good midweek dinner as it is quick to prepare and is lovely with steamed rice. It also makes great rissoles—roll the mixture into patties and pan-fry them until cooked through.

Bring a large saucepan of water to the boil. Fill a large bowl with ice and water. Add half the spinach to the boiling water and cook for 30 seconds, then transfer to the bowl of iced water. Repeat with the remaining spinach.

Drain the spinach and squeeze out all the liquid with your hands. Finely chop the spinach, then put it in a large bowl with the veal, eggs, breadcrumbs and 3 tablespoons of the olive oil. Add the mint, if using, and season with salt and freshly ground black pepper. Mix until well combined. Oil your hands and roll the veal mixture into balls about 55 g (2 oz) each, similar to the size of a golf ball.

Heat the remaining oil in a deep saucepan over medium heat. Cook the meatballs in batches for 2–3 minutes, until light golden brown (do not cook through as they will finish cooking in the sauce). Remove from the pan and set aside.

Add the onion and garlic to the pan and sweat for 3–5 minutes. Add the tomato paste and chilli flakes and cook for another minute. Stir in the chopped tomatoes and stock and bring to the boil. Reduce the heat to medium-low and carefully add the meatballs. Simmer for 25–30 minutes, until the meatballs are cooked through. Season with salt and pepper. Just before serving, stir in the chopped coriander.

2 large bunches English spinach (about 800 g/1 lb 12 oz), trimmed

500 g (1 lb 2 oz) minced (ground) veal

2 eggs

80 g (2¾ oz/⅔ cup) dry breadcrumbs

140 ml (4½ fl oz) olive oil

1 tablespoon dried mint (optional)

1 large brown onion, finely chopped

2 garlic cloves, crushed

4 tablespoons tomato paste (concentrated purée)

1 teaspoon chilli flakes

400 g (14 oz) tin chopped tomatoes

500 ml (17 fl oz/2 cups) beef stock

1 large handful coriander (cilantro), coarsely chopped

SPICE-RUBBED ROAST LEG OF LAMB

SERVES 8

Different rubs make the same main ingredient taste so different. There are plenty of rubs and marinades in chapter seven that you can also use on a leg of lamb (the bastourma rub, Greek-style marinade, all-purpose spice blend, chermola, classic harissa and the yoghurt marinade would all be beautiful with this). I do love using fenugreek and this recipe can also be adapted by adding one tablespoon of powder instead of seeds. For best results I recommend you marinate the leg of lamb in the fridge overnight but if you are pressed for time the minimum would be 4 hours. Bring it to room temperature before cooking.

To make the spicy rub, put all the ingredients in a bowl and mix to combine.

Put the lamb on a rack in a large roasting tin. Using the tip of a sharp knife, make slits in the lamb to allow the rub to flavour the meat. Massage the rub all over the lamb. Marinate in the fridge overnight or for at least 4 hours.

Preheat the oven to 190°C (375°F). Roast the lamb for 20 minutes, then reduce the temperature to 170°C (340°F) and roast for a further 35 minutes. Remove from the oven, cover with baking paper and foil and set aside to rest for at least 20–30 minutes.

To serve, carve the lamb into slices.

2–2.5 kg (4 lb 8 oz–5 lb 8 oz) lamb leg

SPICY RUB

1 teaspoon ground black pepper

3 teaspoons sea salt flakes

3 teaspoons sweet paprika

3 teaspoons fennel seeds, toasted

2 teaspoons ground cumin

2 teaspoons ground coriander

2 teaspoons chilli flakes

5 cm (2 inch) piece ginger, grated

grated zest of 1 lemon

4 garlic cloves

160 ml (5¼ fl oz) olive oil

BAKED RAINBOW TROUT WITH TAHINI AND PINE NUTS

SERVES 4

Growing up beside the beach, we used to be able to get a lot of fresh fish from the local port. Cooking fish was the one thing my mum wasn't very good at doing in the kitchen, but somehow she was capable of perfecting this dish.

Preheat the oven to 190°C (375°F). Line a baking tray with baking paper.

Put the rainbow trout on the tray. Drizzle with the oil and season with salt and freshly ground black pepper. Bake for 15–20 minutes, until done to your liking.

Put the tahini in a bowl with the garlic and 250 ml (9 fl oz/1 cup) water. Season with salt and whisk until smooth. Pour this mixture over the cooked fish and bake for 1 minute, just until the tahini is lukewarm (overheating the tahini will cause it to curdle).

Serve the fish garnished with the pine nuts, parsley and chilli.

2 rainbow trout, about 450–500 g (1 lb–1 lb 2 oz) each, scaled and gutted

4 tablespoons olive oil

270 g (9½ oz/1 cup) tahini

2 garlic cloves, crushed

4 tablespoons pine nuts, toasted

3 tablespoons chopped flat-leaf (Italian) parsley

1 large fresh red chilli, finely chopped

SAGE-ROASTED CHICKEN

SERVES 4–6

Stuffed chicken was one of my favourite childhood dishes. This is a modernised, fancier version of the dish Mum used to cook. I find the sage gives the chicken a fragrant aroma that fills the whole house while it's roasting. If you don't like sage, you can use rosemary or any other type of sturdy herb.

Preheat the oven to 190°C (375°F). Line a roasting tin with baking paper.

Wash the chicken and pat dry with paper towel. Set the chicken aside at room temperature while you prepare the stuffing.

To make the stuffing, heat the oil in a frying pan over medium heat. Cook the onion for 5 minutes, or until lightly golden. Add the veal and season with salt and freshly ground black pepper. Cook for 8–10 minutes, until the veal is cooked through. Remove from the heat and set aside to cool. Add the pine nuts and chopped sage leaves and mix together.

Stuff the chicken cavity with the veal mixture.

Combine the lemon zest with the olive oil, sea salt and cracked pepper, then rub the mixture over the whole chicken.

Spread the bunches of sage over the base of the roasting tin, then place the stuffed chicken on top. Bake for 45–50 minutes, until the chicken is cooked through.

1 large free-range chicken, around 1.5 kg (3 lb 5 oz)

grated zest of 1 lemon

100 ml (3½ fl oz) olive oil

sea salt and cracked black pepper, for seasoning

5 bunches sage, for roasting

STUFFING

2 tablespoons olive oil

1 small brown onion, finely chopped

120 g (4¼ oz) minced (ground) veal

4 tablespoons pine nuts, lightly toasted

15 sage leaves, finely chopped

SLOW-ROASTED LAMB SHOULDER

SERVES 6–8

We like to eat a lot of Asian food at home, so I've used that as inspiration for this slow-roasted lamb, which is rubbed with an Asian-inspired curry paste. You can also use the paste with chicken, fish and vegetables. Although slow-cooked meats are typically served in cooler months, this dish is great all year round because the sauce isn't too heavy.

To make the curry paste, put the toasted coriander and cumin seeds in a food processor and blitz to break down. Add the lemon zest, ginger, garlic, chilli, coriander leaves and stems, olive oil and salt. Blitz until the mixture is combined.

Put the lamb shoulder in a large bowl and cover with the curry paste. Marinate in the fridge for at least 4–6 hours, but preferably overnight for the best flavour.

Preheat the oven to 180°C (350°F).

Scrape the paste off the lamb shoulder and set aside in a bowl. Heat the oil in a frying pan over medium heat. Sear the lamb on all sides until browned. Add the reserved paste to the pan and cook for 2–3 minutes.

Transfer the lamb to a deep roasting tin with a lid. Add the stock and tomato and bring to the boil on the stovetop. Cover and transfer to the oven to cook for 1 hour. Reduce the temperature to 160°C (320°F) and cook for a further 4 hours, occasionally basting the lamb with the sauce and checking there is enough liquid. Add more stock if needed.

Remove the lid and skim off any excess oil. Cook the lamb for another 20 minutes, or until the sauce has reduced and thickened.

Serve the roasted lamb straight from the roasting tin. It should be tender enough that it can be torn off in chunks.

1 lamb shoulder, bone in, about 1.5–1.8 kg (3 lb 5 oz–4 lb)

4 tablespoons olive oil

250 ml (9 fl oz/1 cup) beef stock, plus extra, if needed

2 x 400 g (14 oz) tins chopped tomatoes

CURRY PASTE

2 tablespoons coriander seeds, lightly toasted

2 tablespoons cumin seeds, lightly toasted

grated zest of 1 lemon

2 cm (¾ inch) piece ginger, coarsely chopped

2 garlic cloves

2 small fresh red chillies, coarsely chopped

1 large handful coriander (cilantro)

125 ml (4 fl oz/½ cup) olive oil

1 tablespoon salt

VEAL MEATBALLS WITH SPINACH & LEMON BROTH

SERVES 4

You can't go past a good meatball soup for a Sunday night dinner. If you don't have burghul in the pantry, it can be replaced with dry breadcrumbs—just skip the soaking step if you use those.

Put the burghul in a fine sieve and rinse under very hot water for about 30 seconds. Press lightly to remove any excess liquid, then spread the burghul out in a large bowl to cool.

Add the veal, onion, paprika and cumin to the burghul and season with salt and freshly ground black pepper. Use your hands to mix until well combined. Lightly oil your hands to prevent sticking, then roll the veal mixture into golf ball-sized rounds, about 30 g (1 oz) each. Set aside.

To make the broth, heat the oil in a large saucepan over medium heat. Sauté the onion, garlic and celery for 3–5 minutes, until transparent. Add the coriander seeds and turmeric and sauté for another minute. Pour in the stock and bring to the boil over high heat.

Reduce the heat to a simmer and add the meatballs, gently shaking the pan so the meatballs settle into a single layer. Cook for 25–30 minutes, skimming occasionally but taking care not to remove all the coriander seeds, until the meatballs are cooked through. Add the spinach and cook briefly until wilted. Stir in the lemon juice and season with salt and pepper.

100 g (3½ oz) fine burghul (bulgur)
500 g (1 lb 2 oz) coarsely minced (ground) veal
1 small brown onion, finely diced
1 tablespoon sweet paprika
2 tablespoons ground cumin
olive oil, for rolling

BROTH
3 tablespoons olive oil
1 brown onion, finely diced
2 garlic cloves, finely chopped
3 celery stalks, halved lengthways and finely chopped
2 tablespoons coriander seeds, lightly toasted
1½ tablespoons ground turmeric
1.5 litres (52 fl oz/6 cups) chicken stock
2 bunches English spinach, coarsely chopped
juice of ½ lemon

CHAPTER FOUR

WARM VEGETABLES

Unfortunately, too many people make boring choices when it comes to the vegetables they serve with their mains. And they seem to eat those steamed or boiled veg out of a sense of duty rather than for enjoyment. For me, the opposite has always been true. As a child, the grilled tomatoes and onions left over after a barbecue were the real treat. Any spare eggplant would be turned into baba ghanoush for sandwiches the next day, and it was something we looked forward to.

When Kristy and I cook, the vegetables on our dinner table are given the same care as the meat dishes—they aren't an afterthought. Something as simple as putting tahini, salt and cumin on a cauliflower before roasting it can turn it into the most delicious thing on the table. A few slivered almonds and some crumbled goat's cheese over steamed beans makes them irresistible. I always start with the vegetable dishes then move to the meat, not because I 'have' to, but because that's what I like. We hope this chapter helps expand your vegetable horizons.

ASPARAGUS, BLACK OLIVES AND TOMATOES

SERVES 4–6 AS A SIDE DISH

We eat a lot of vegetables in our house and often when we have a delicious piece of steak for dinner, the vegetables are eaten before the meat. We love a variety of warm vegetables with our meals and this dish is great served with meat or fish.

Trim and peel the asparagus spears and set aside.

Heat the oil in a large frying pan over medium heat. Sauté the garlic until transparent. Add the chilli and cook for 1 minute or until fragrant. Add the tomato and increase the heat to high. Cook for 4–5 minutes, until the tomato is almost breaking apart. Add the olives and season with salt and freshly ground black pepper. Add the spring onion, then remove from the heat and keep hot.

Bring a large saucepan of water to the boil and, once boiling, blanch the asparagus for about 10 seconds, then drain and refresh immediately in cold water. Alternatively, heat a barbecue or chargrill pan to high. Lightly brush the asparagus with the extra oil and season with salt and pepper. Cook until done to your liking.

Transfer the cooked asparagus to a platter and spoon the tomato and olive mixture on top.

NOTE

You can blanch the asparagus in boiling water for 10 seconds instead of barbecuing it.

Pictured on page 89

36 asparagus spears, about 3 bunches

3 tablespoons olive oil, plus 2 tablespoons for brushing, if needed

2 garlic cloves, crushed

1 small fresh green chilli, finely chopped

3 large tomatoes, finely diced

100 g (3½ oz) pitted black olives, halved

30 g (1 oz/½ cup) chopped spring onions (scallions)

SILVERBEET WITH HARISSA

SERVES 4–6 AS A SIDE DISH

Eating greens that have been lightly steamed with a bit of seasoning makes me feel so healthy. Asian food does this really well so I've applied that style of preparation to this dish. The silverbeet has a good crunch to it and the spicy hit from the harissa makes this a gutsy vegetable dish. It's best served with a protein, like steak—something that can hold its own against these bold flavours.

Thoroughly wash the silverbeet to remove any soil and grit, then coarsely chop the leaves and stems.

Heat the oil in a large frying pan over medium heat. Sauté the onion and garlic for 4–5 minutes, until lightly golden.

Meanwhile, blanch the silverbeet in a saucepan of boiling water for 1 minute, then drain. Do not overcook the silverbeet—it should still be quite green and firm.

Add the drained silverbeet and harissa to the frying pan with the onion and garlic and gently toss for 1 minute. Season with salt and freshly ground black pepper, then fold in the pecans and serve.

Pictured on page 88

1 large bunch silverbeet (Swiss chard)

100 ml (3½ fl oz) olive oil

1 brown onion, finely chopped

3 garlic cloves, finely chopped

30 g (1 oz) harissa

100 g (3½ oz/1 cup) pecans, lightly toasted

1. ROASTED PUMPKIN WITH DUKKAH AND MINTED YOGHURT see page 131
2. GREEN BEANS WITH GOAT'S CHEESE, ALMONDS AND LEMON see page 130
3. ROAST CHICKEN WITH SOURDOUGH STUFFING see page 86
4. ROASTED WHOLE BABY CAULIFLOWER see page 138

GREEN BEANS WITH GOAT'S CHEESE, ALMONDS AND LEMON

SERVES 4–6 AS A SIDE DISH

Kristy cooks dinner most Sunday nights as it's the end of a busy week of cooking for me. One of my favourite meals she cooks is barbecued steak with a few different vegetables, and this is one of her best recipes. The lemon zest and goat's cheese almost melt together to make the most delicious topping, taking the beans to a new level.

Blanch the beans in a saucepan of boiling water for 1–2 minutes, until done to your liking. Drain well and shake off any excess water.

Put the lemon zest and olive oil in a large bowl. Add the beans and toss to coat.

Transfer the hot beans to a serving dish and top with the goat's cheese and toasted almonds.

Pictured on page 128

500 g (1 lb 2 oz) green beans, topped and tailed
grated zest of 1½ lemons
olive oil, for drizzling
100 g (3½ oz) marinated goat's cheese
50 g (1¾ oz) slivered almonds, lightly toasted

ROASTED PUMPKIN WITH DUKKAH AND MINTED YOGHURT

SERVES 6 AS A SIDE DISH

Adding dukkah before roasting is a great way to boost the flavour of—as well as provide crunch and texture to—the humble pumpkin. It makes a great main course for vegetarians and is pretty delicious the next day if there's any left over

Preheat the oven to 190°C (375°F). Line a large baking tray with baking paper.

Cut the pumpkin into large wedges, leaving the skin on. Transfer to a large bowl with the olive oil and salt and toss to combine. Spread the pumpkin on the baking tray and sprinkle with the dukkah. Bake for 15–20 minutes, until the pumpkin is golden and tender.

Meanwhile, to make the dressing, combine the yoghurt, olive oil and mint in a small bowl and season with salt, to taste. Sprinkle the lemon zest over the top.

Arrange the pumpkin wedges on a platter and serve hot or at room temperature, with the dressing alongside.

Pictured on page 128

1 large butternut pumpkin (squash)
100 ml (3½ fl oz) olive oil
1 teaspoon sea salt flakes
50 g (1¾ oz) hazelnut dukkah (page 228)

DRESSING
100 g (3½ oz) Greek-style yoghurt
2 tablespoons extra virgin olive oil
1 large handful mint, leaves picked and chopped
grated zest of 1 lemon

SUGAR SNAP PEAS WITH SUJUK AND HAZELNUTS

SERVES 4 AS A SIDE DISH

I first made this dish for Christmas lunch and it was a big hit with our guests. The sujuk and hazelnuts transform this humble green vegetable into an into an amazing side dish.

Heat the oil in a frying pan over medium heat. Add the chopped sujuk and cook for 4–5 minutes, until crisp.

Blanch the sugar snap peas in a large saucepan of boiling water for 2 minutes, or until they are done to your liking, then drain.

Add the sugar snap peas to the frying pan and sauté with the sujuk for 1 minute. Add the chopped hazelnuts and parsley and mix until combined. Season with freshly cracked black pepper, then taste and add salt if needed.

NOTE

Sujuk is a spicy Mediterranean-style sausage available from Middle Eastern grocers or butchers. You can substitute one hot chorizo sausage for the sujuk.

2 tablespoons olive oil

200 g (7 oz) sujuk sausage, finely chopped (see Note)

500 g (1 lb 2 oz) sugar snap peas, trimmed

80 g (2¾ oz) hazelnuts, toasted, skinned and coarsely chopped

1 handful flat-leaf (Italian) parsley, finely chopped

GRILLED BRUSSELS SPROUTS WITH MANCHEGO

SERVES 4–6 AS A SIDE DISH

I know I shouldn't be lecturing people about brussels sprouts, especially since I wasn't raised eating them and that's probably why I like them. I cook them a little differently to most people, creating the perfect combination of sweet, salty and spicy. If you're one of the many yet to be convinced about this vegetable, give this a try.

Bring a large saucepan of water to the boil over high heat. Blanch the brussels sprouts for 1–2 minutes, until bright green but still firm, then drain and set aside.

To make the honey glaze, combine the olive oil, honey and chilli flakes in a bowl. Season with salt and freshly ground black pepper.

Add the brussels sprouts to the honey glaze and toss to coat.

Heat a chargrill pan or barbecue to medium–high. Cook the brussels sprouts for 1 minute on each side, or until done to your liking. The honey will start to burn fairly quickly.

Put the charred brussels sprouts on a platter or in a serving bowl. Sprinkle with the crispy shallots and garlic. Grate the manchego cheese over the top (it will melt slightly from the heat of the brussels sprouts) and serve.

500 g (1 lb 2 oz) small brussels sprouts, trimmed
50 g (1¾ oz) crispy fried shallots
2 tablespoons crispy fried garlic
50 g (1¾ oz) manchego cheese

HONEY GLAZE
100 ml (3½ fl oz) olive oil
3 tablespoons honey
½ teaspoon chilli flakes

BROCCOLINI PANGRATTATO

SERVES 4 AS A SIDE DISH

Pangrattato is a classic Italian seasoning that works really well with vegetables. I've served it with steamed broccolini here but it would also work well with cauliflower, beans or even as a crumble topping for mashed sweet potato. It is based on crisp breadcrumbs and this one also has almonds to give it more crunch and texture.

Heat the oil in a frying pan over medium heat. Add the chopped almonds, breadcrumbs and anchovy fillets. Cook, stirring, until the breadcrumbs are golden and the anchovies break down. Add the salt, pepper and sage leaves. Set aside in the frying pan.

Put the broccolini into a large saucepan of boiling water. Blanch for 1–2 minutes, until bright green and tender, then drain.

While the broccolini is cooking, return the frying pan with the pangrattato mixture to medium heat. Add the drained broccolini and toss it through the pangrattato mixture.

3 tablespoons light olive oil

50 g (1¾ oz) almonds, lightly toasted and coarsely chopped

50 g (1¾ oz) dry breadcrumbs

4 anchovy fillets

1 teaspoon sea salt flakes

½ teaspoon cracked black pepper

10 large sage leaves, finely chopped

2 bunches broccolini, trimmed

STEAMED LEEKS WITH SPINACH AND HALOUMI

SERVES 4 AS A SIDE DISH

Leeks are underrated vegetables that can easily be a hero in their own right. They don't necessarily have to be chopped up in soups or stews—try adding a few ingredients as I've done here to make the leek into a dish of its own

Thoroughly wash the leeks and cut them into 5 cm (2 inch) pieces.

Melt the butter in a frying pan over medium heat. Fry the sage leaves for 2–3 minutes, until they are fragrant but not browned. Reduce the heat to low and add the leek pieces standing upright. Cover and steam for 6 minutes.

Season the leek with salt and freshly ground black pepper. Scatter the spinach leaves over the top, cover and steam for a further 2 minutes. Sprinkle with the grated haloumi or parmesan and serve.

NOTE

The leeks need to be thoroughly washed as they often contain a lot of soil and grit. Try to preserve their shape when you are washing them.

3 leeks, pale part only

30 g (1 oz) butter

10 sage leaves

100 g (3½ oz/2¼ cups) baby English spinach

30 g (1 oz) haloumi or parmesan cheese, finely grated

ROASTED WHOLE BABY CAULIFLOWER

SERVES 6–8 AS A SIDE DISH

Cauliflower can be perceived as boring, but the thing that makes vegetables interesting is the way they are cooked. I like cooking this dish in a wood-fired oven but it works just as well in a regular oven at home. You can serve the cauliflower with a crisp lettuce salad as a vegetarian meal and you can certainly impress guests by serving it as a side dish.

Preheat the oven to 190°C (375°F).

Blanch the whole cauliflower in a large saucepan of boiling water for 4–5 minutes, then drain.

Combine the cumin, olive oil and 1 tablespoon of the sea salt flakes to make a runny paste. Massage this mixture all over each cauliflower. Put the cauliflower on a baking tray and roast for 25–30 minutes, until golden and tender.

Transfer the cauliflower to a serving plate, drizzle with the tahini and sprinkle with the cumin seeds, pepper, remaining sea salt and parsley.

NOTE

Depending on the size of your saucepan, you may need to boil the cauliflower one at a time.

Pictured on page 129

2 small heads baby cauliflower, about 450 g (1 lb) each

2 tablespoons ground cumin

125 ml (4 fl oz/½ cup) olive oil, plus extra for drizzling

1½ tablespoons sea salt flakes

135 g (4¾ oz/½ cup) raw tahini

1 tablespoon cumin seeds, toasted and crushed

2 teaspoons ground black pepper

2 tablespoons chopped flat-leaf (Italian) parsley

ROASTED FENNEL WITH PARMESAN AND SAGE

SERVES 4–6 AS A SIDE DISH

Fennel is quite a polarising vegetable because the aniseed flavour can turn people off. But roasting the fennel makes it sweet and soft, and having the cheese and sage bubbling on top gives it a lovely crust. Even so-called 'fennel haters' will be back for more.

Preheat the oven to 180°C (350°F). Line a large baking tray with baking paper.

Put the butter, oil, sage and parmesan in a bowl and mix to combine. Season with salt and freshly ground black pepper. Add the fennel pieces and use your hands to coat them with the sage mixture.

Spread the fennel on the baking tray in a single layer and bake for 30–35 minutes, until golden brown.

20 g (¾ oz) butter, at room temperature

2 tablespoons olive oil

8 sage leaves, finely chopped

3 tablespoons grated parmesan cheese

2 fennel bulbs, trimmed and cut into eighths

SCORCHED ONIONS WITH POMEGRANATE MOLASSES AND HALOUMI

SERVES 4–6 AS A SIDE DISH

Scorched onions are a childhood favourite of mine and they always remind me of a barbecue gathering. The pomegranate adds a lovely sweetness and acidity that makes this recipe work well as a side dish with any grilled meat or fish.

Preheat the oven to 180°C (350°F).

Heat a chargrill pan to high. Put the onion halves in a bowl and toss with the olive oil. Put the onions in the chargrill pan, cut side down, and cook for 4–5 minutes without turning, until grill marks appear. Turn the onions over and then transfer to the oven for 5 minutes to finish cooking.

Transfer the onions to a serving plate or platter and drizzle with the pomegranate molasses. Shave the haloumi over the top and serve.

5 small red onions, halved crosswise

3 tablespoons olive oil

2 tablespoons pomegranate molasses

50 g (1¾ oz) haloumi cheese

ZUCCHINI CHIPS

SERVES 2–4 AS A SNACK

This is more of a snack than a side dish, but if you crave potato chips (crisps), this is a much healthier alternative. They take a little bit more work than buying a packet from a shop, and yes, they do take an hour to bake, but they are so easy to prepare and absolutely delicious.

Preheat the oven to 100°C (200°F). Line 2 large baking trays with baking paper.

Lay the zucchini slices on the trays in a single layer. Lightly drizzle with olive oil, sprinkle with sea salt and chilli flakes, if using.

Bake for 1 hour, or until the zucchini is crisp. Do not allow it to brown too much or the chips will be bitter. Serve immediately.

Pictured opposite

2–3 zucchini (courgettes), thinly sliced
olive oil, for drizzling
sea salt flakes
chilli flakes (optional)

SWEET POTATO CHIPS

SERVES 4–6 AS A SIDE DISH

As much as we love deep-fried, deliciously salty hot chips, they are not very good for us. These sweet potato chips are a good alternative as they are baked in the oven. The spices and sugar give them a delicious crisp texture.

Preheat the oven to 180°C (350°F). Line a large baking tray with baking paper.

Put the olive oil, coriander, cumin, sea salt and brown sugar in a large bowl and mix to combine. Add the sweet potato batons and use your hands to coat the sweet potato with the spice mixture.

Scatter the sweet potato chips over the baking tray and spread out in a single layer. Bake for 1 hour, or until golden and crisp.

100 ml (3½ fl oz) olive oil
1 teaspoon ground coriander
1 teaspoon ground cumin
1 teaspoon sea salt flakes
1 tablespoon light brown sugar
1 kg (2 lb 4 oz) orange sweet potato, peeled and cut into thick batons

CHAPTER FIVE

HOT TEAS & ICED TEAS

Whether it's a hot cup of tea in the morning, or a mint tea to signify the end of a meal, we love these little rituals. Most people think of tea as a drink served hot, often with milk. Like coffee, the tea culture is a big part of café life here in Australia and around the world. The teas that we serve in our two restaurants are as important as the coffee. Working with our bar manager, Ladislav Smid, we've created a selection of hot and cold tea recipes that can all be made and enjoyed at home. If you're having people over for brunch or a party, beautiful jugs of iced teas are a wonderful alternative to coffee or alcohol. They also add beauty to the table with very little effort.

CARDAMOM TEA

MAKES 500 ML (17 FL OZ/2 CUPS)

In the Middle East, green cardamom powder is used as a spice for sweet dishes as well as being a traditional flavouring. Green cardamom is also a common ingredient in Indian cooking, and is used in traditional Indian sweets and in tea or chai. I think this tea has magical healing powers.

Pour 600 ml (21 fl oz) water into a saucepan and add the cardamom pods, peppercorns, cloves, cinnamon sticks and ginger. Bring to a simmer over medium–low heat, then simmer for 30 minutes.

Strain the tea into teacups and serve with the honey or sugar and milk, to taste.

8 cardamom pods
8 black peppercorns
8 cloves
2 cinnamon sticks
3 cm (1¼ inch) piece ginger, thinly sliced
honey or sugar, to serve
milk, to serve

SAGE TEA

MAKES 1 LITRE (35 FL OZ/4 CUPS)

Sage is a desert herb native to the Mediterranean. It has a distinct flavour and aroma, and it also offers a number of potential health and medicinal benefits. I was usually served this classic Middle Eastern tea by my Nana when I wasn't feeling well.

Put the sage leaves in a teapot, pour in the boiling water and steep for 3–5 minutes.

Add the lemon slices and honey to the tea and infuse for 1 minute, then strain and serve.

4 sage sprigs
1 litre (35 fl oz/4 cups) boiling water
2 lemon slices
3 teaspoons honey

EGYPTIAN HIBISCUS ICED TEA WITH LEMON

MAKES 1 LITRE (35 FL OZ/4 CUPS)

Egyptian hibiscus iced tea is the most popular iced tea that we serve at Kepos & Co. Coffee has always been big in Australia, so we wanted to highlight the importance of tea, both cold and hot. We use dried hibiscus flower heads with a light Ceylon orange pekoe tea, but you can also buy hibiscus tea from most Middle Eastern grocers. The hibiscus offers a lovely tartness and is well balanced by the black tea—it's a cooling and refreshing tea in the hot months.

Put the tea leaves in a large teapot or saucepan, pour in the boiling water and steep for 4–5 minutes. Strain the tea into a heatproof pitcher and discard the tea leaves.

Add the lemon slices and sugar syrup, to taste. Cover and chill the tea until ready to serve.

1½ tablespoons hibiscus tea leaves
1 litre (35 fl oz/4 cups) boiling water
1 lemon, sliced
sugar syrup (page 245), to taste

STRAWBERRY TEA WITH ROSEWATER

MAKES 1.2 LITRES (42 FL OZ)

This is a tea that our Kepos Bar Manager and I created. I'm not sure that it has any medicinal benefits, but the colour, fragrance and taste definitely make me happy. To me, anything that makes me feel happy is of medicinal benefit.

Put the dried strawberries and 1.5 litres (52 fl oz/6 cups) of water in a saucepan. Bring to the boil over medium heat, then reduce the heat to low and simmer for 15 minutes.

Strain the hot tea into a clear glass teapot. Add the honey, rosewater, rose petals, orange zest and fresh strawberry slices. Stir to combine.

NOTE

You can use packaged dried strawberries or you can dry strawberries at home using a dehydrator or the oven. You will need 500 g (1 lb 2 oz) of fresh strawberries for this recipe. Wash the strawberries and let them drain in a colander for a few minutes. Slice off and discard the hulls, then slice the strawberries so the pieces are all approximately the same thickness—the direction that you slice them is less important than the thickness. Arrange the strawberry slices on the dehydrator trays or baking trays so that there is at least 1 cm (½ inch) between the slices.

Set the dehydrator or oven temperature to 70°C (150°F). The strawberries will take 8–10 hours to dry fully or 10–14 hours if you want them to be crisp rather than pliable. The pieces should feel completely dry to the touch.

You won't know if the strawberry pieces are fully dehydrated until they have cooled. Turn off the dehydrator and open it, or remove the baking trays from the oven. Let the strawberries cool for 20–30 minutes, then break one of the pieces in half. There should be no visible moisture along the surface of the break.

200 g (7 oz) sliced dried strawberries (see Note)

2 teaspoons honey

1 teaspoon rosewater

2 tablespoons edible dried rose petals

1 large strip orange zest

2 fresh strawberries, sliced

MIDDLE EASTERN MASALA CHAI

MAKES 1 LITRE (35 FL OZ/4 CUPS)

Masala chai is a flavoured tea made by brewing black tea with a mixture of aromatic Indian spices and herbs. Originating in India, it has gained popularity and become a feature in many Western cafés and restaurants. It is traditionally prepared by combining green cardamom pods, cinnamon sticks, ground cloves, ground ginger and black peppercorns with black tea leaves. In the Middle East, particularly in the countries surrounding the Persian Gulf where it is highly popular, the drink is commonly called 'karak chai' by the locals and this is my version of the traditional tea.

Heat a frying pan over medium heat and lightly toast the cloves, cardamom pods, star anise, peppercorns and fennel seeds until fragrant. Crush the spices using a mortar and pestle until they form a coarse mixture.

Pour 700 ml (24 fl oz) water into a heavy-based saucepan and bring to the boil. Add the toasted spices, cinnamon stick, ground cinnamon, vanilla bean halves, saffron, aniseed, nutmeg, ginger and tea leaves and infuse in the boiling water for 2–3 minutes. Pour in the milk and heat through. Pour the mixture into a teapot and stir in the honey.

The flavour will intensify the longer the tea is left to infuse. Strain the tea before serving.

4 cloves

5 cardamom pods, lightly crushed

3 star anise

½ teaspoon black peppercorns

¼ teaspoon fennel seeds

1 cinnamon stick

¼ teaspoon ground cinnamon

1 vanilla bean, split lengthways

pinch of saffron threads

¼ teaspoon whole aniseed

¼ whole nutmeg, grated

⅓ teaspoon ground ginger

3 tablespoons loose black tea leaves

300 ml (10½ fl oz) cow's milk or soy milk

1 tablespoon honey

ANISEED TEA

MAKES 1.2 LITRES (42 FL OZ)

Now this is a tea that I've been making for a long time. Not only does it taste great, it has a mild soothing quality—it's certainly nothing medicinal, but enjoying a few moments of peaceful sipping in a busy day can't be a bad thing. The seeds of the anise plant carry a sweet fragrance and an almost liquorice-like flavour. Originally grown in Egypt and the Mediterranean, anise is now used all over the world.

Add the cinnamon sticks and star anise to a teapot, pour in the boiling water and infuse for 3–4 minutes.

Put the tea leaves in an infuser, then add to the teapot with the lemon slices and infuse for a further 1–2 minutes. Remove the infuser, add the honey and sugar and stir to combine.

2 cinnamon sticks

4 star anise

1.2 litres (42 fl oz) boiling water

2 tablespoons black tea leaves

½ lemon, sliced

2 tablespoons honey

1 teaspoon sugar

PERSIAN TEA

MAKES 1 LITRE (35 FL OZ/4 CUPS)

When you are welcomed into a Persian home, the first thing you are offered is a hot, well-brewed cup of tea. Tea is the hot drink of choice for most people in Iran, where it is served for breakfast, lunch, dinner and in between, with at least one or more refills.

Pour 1 litre (35 fl oz/4 cups) of water into a saucepan and add the rosewater, cardamom pods and cinnamon sticks. Bring to the boil over medium-low heat, then reduce the heat to low and simmer for 30 minutes to infuse the flavours into the water.

Put the tea leaves in a teapot. Bring the infused water to the boil, pour into the teapot and steep for 2–3 minutes.

Strain the tea into tea glasses and serve with the honey and milk, to taste.

NOTE

You can serve this tea with sugar cubes, dates, raisins or other sweets. However, for serious tea drinkers, adding sugar, milk or anything else would detract from the taste of the tea.

1 teaspoon rosewater

2–3 cardamom pods, opened

2 small cinnamon sticks

2 tablespoons black tea leaves, preferably assam

honey, to serve

milk, to serve

TURKISH APPLE TEA

MAKES ABOUT 1 LITRE (35 FL OZ/4 CUPS)

When slowly brewed on the stove in the traditional style, the dried apples release their natural sweetness. This caffeine-free tea is as impressive and addictive cold as it is hot. It's the most fruity and truly delicious tea and a great substitute for a dessert. Take the refreshing taste to another level by adding a few fresh mint sprigs to each glass.

Put the dried apples, cinnamon sticks, cloves and 800 ml (28 fl oz) of water in a saucepan. Bring to the boil over medium heat, then reduce the heat to low and simmer for 15 minutes.

Strain the hot tea into a teapot, gently pushing on the apples with a spoon to extract all the liquid. Sweeten the tea with the honey, then pour into tea glasses and serve.

200 g (7 oz) dried apple slices
2 cinnamon sticks
4 cloves
1 teaspoon honey

MOROCCAN MINT TEA

MAKES 1 LITRE (35 FL OZ/4 CUPS)

This tea brings back so many childhood and adult memories for me. 'Nana' is the Hebrew word for mint, and Moroccan-style mint tea is so loved and so common in Israel that it's practically been adopted as a national signature drink. It's a beautiful palate cleanser and an amazing digestif after any meal.

To make the Moroccan mint tea leaves, mix the tea and dried mint leaves until combined.

Put 4 tablespoons of the Moroccan mint tea leaves in an infuser, then place in a teapot. Pour in the boiling water, add the fresh mint leaves and infuse for 2 minutes. Add sugar, to taste.

NOTE

Store any leftover Moroccan mint tea leaves in an airtight container for up to 6 months. They can also be packaged and given as a gift.

Pictured on page 23

1 litre (35 fl oz/4 cups) boiling water
2 mint sprigs, leaves picked
sugar, to taste

MOROCCAN MINT TEA LEAVES

10 g (¼ oz) silver jasmine or green gunpowder tea
20 g (¾ oz) dried mint leaves

GOLDEN PEONY AND PEAR ICED TEA WITH VANILLA

MAKES 1 LITRE (35 FL OZ/4 CUPS)

If you enjoy commercial iced teas, this tea is for you. It is a much healthier, less processed and more fragrant version. I love the combination of the white tea with the fresh pears and the scent of the vanilla bean.

Core the pears, cut them into cubes and place in a large container. Crush with a muddler or the end of a rolling pin until the skin of the pears has broken. Add the vanilla bean and set aside.

Put the tea leaves in a large teapot or saucepan, pour in the hot water and steep for 3 minutes.

Pour the tea over the pear mixture through a fine strainer and discard the tea leaves. Leave the pear mixture at room temperature for at least 1 hour, or overnight if possible.

Pour the tea through the strainer into a large pitcher, discarding the pear and vanilla bean. Add the sugar syrup, to taste. Cover and chill the tea until ready to serve. Garnish with pear slices.

NOTE

The water should be hot but not boiling, approximately 80°C (175°F).

2 pears, plus extra pear slices, to garnish

½ vanilla bean, split

2½ tablespoons golden peony or other white tea leaves

1 litre (35 fl oz/4 cups) hot water (see Note)

sugar syrup (page 245), to taste

IRON GODDESS ICED TEA WITH PLUMS, MINT AND LEMON LEAVES

MAKES ABOUT 1.25 LITRES (44 FL OZ/5 CUPS)

Iron goddess is a Chinese tea known for its signature floral scent and it's one of those teas that doesn't like the temperature of boiling water—hot water does the job. If you can't find lemon leaves, lime leaves will work just as well.

Put the plums in a large container. Crush with a muddler or the end of a rolling pin until the skins have broken (leave the stones in). Add the mint and lemon leaves and set aside.

Put the tea leaves in a large teapot or saucepan, pour in the hot water and steep for 3 minutes.

Pour the tea over the plum mixture through a fine strainer and discard the tea leaves. Leave the plum mixture at room temperature for at least 1 hour, or overnight if possible.

Pour the tea through the strainer into a large pitcher, discarding the plums, stones and leaves. Add the sugar syrup, to taste. Cover and chill the tea until ready to serve. Garnish with the fresh mint leaves and plum slices, if using.

NOTE

The water should be hot but not boiling, approximately 80°C (175°F).

4 plums, plus extra plum slices, to garnish (optional)

1 mint sprig, plus extra to garnish

5 lemon leaves

1½ tablespoons iron goddess or oolong tea leaves

1 litre (35 fl oz/4 cups) hot water (see Note)

sugar syrup (page 245), to taste

LAVENDER AND PEACH ICED TEA WITH HONEY

MAKES 1 LITRE (35 FL OZ/4 CUPS)

Lavender is an acquired taste but I highly recommend trying this fragrant iced tea. Make it in summer when peaches are in season and at their sweetest and ripest.

2 peaches, plus extra peach slices, to garnish

1 teaspoon honey, or to taste

2½ tablespoons lavender tea (see Note)

1 litre (35 fl oz/4 cups) boiling water

mint leaves, to garnish (optional)

Cut the peaches in half, discard the stones, then cut the flesh into cubes and place in a large heatproof container. Crush with a muddler or the end of a rolling pin until the skin of the peaches has broken. Add the honey and set aside.

Put the tea leaves in a large teapot or saucepan, pour in the boiling water and steep for 4–5 minutes.

Pour the tea over the peach mixture through a fine strainer and discard the tea leaves. Leave the peach mixture at room temperature for at least 1 hour, or overnight if possible.

Pour the tea through the strainer into a large pitcher and discard the peaches. Cover and chill until ready to serve. Garnish with peach slices or mint leaves, if using.

NOTE

Make your own lavender tea by combining 1½ tablespoons black tea with 3 teaspoons edible dried lavender. I use lavender flower heads with a light Ceylon orange pekoe tea.

ORANGE PEKOE BERRY ICED TEA

MAKES 1 LITRE (35 FL OZ/4 CUPS)

This is one of my favourite iced teas. It's a beautiful combination of tea and fruit juice and a really refreshing drink on a hot day.

30 g (1 oz) strawberries

30 g (1 oz) raspberries

30 g (1 oz) blueberries

1 star anise

2 cinnamon sticks

2 tablespoons orange pekoe tea leaves

1 litre (35 fl oz/4 cups) boiling water

sugar syrup (page 245), to taste

Combine all the berries in large heatproof container and lightly crush them with a muddler or the end of a rolling pin until the juices start to come out. Add the star anise and cinnamon sticks and set aside.

Put the tea leaves in a large teapot or saucepan, pour in the boiling water and steep for 4–5 minutes.

Pour the tea over the berry mixture through a fine strainer and discard the tea leaves. Leave the berry mixture at room temperature for at least 1 hour, or overnight if possible.

Pour the tea through the strainer into a large pitcher and discard the berries. Add the sugar syrup, to taste. Cover and chill the tea until ready to serve.

NOTE

The tea can be garnished with extra berries, if desired.

CHAPTER SIX

SWEETS

I loved working on this chapter because I have a big sweet tooth (actually, I have an everything tooth—I don't discriminate!). Middle Eastern desserts tend to be very sweet and syrupy (baklava, for example), and they are enjoyed at various points of the day rather than after a big meal. If you have guests over, you might serve dried fruits, nuts and mint tea after dinner, but not cake—that's a very Western thing.

In this chapter, we've married the Western idea of dessert after dinner with the Middle Eastern flavour palate. There are sweet treats to serve during the day, such as Pistachio frangipane slice and then delicious desserts like the Layered Turkish delight pavlova or the impressive Banana kataifi tarte tatin. And, of course, there's Churros—the Kepos Street Kitchen signature dessert. Always a favourite.

DATES STUFFED WITH GOAT'S CHEESE AND PISTACHIOS

MAKES 20

When you run out of time and still want an impressive dessert, this is definitely a winner. It doesn't require much effort and there is zero cooking time. You could leave out the sugar and honey and serve this as a savoury dish when guests arrive. It's also a lovely addition to a cheese board.

Put the goat's cheese, milk and sugar in a bowl and mix with a spoon to soften the goat's cheese. Spoon the mixture into a piping (icing) bag and use it to fill the dates.

Arrange the stuffed dates on a serving plate. Scatter the pistachios over the top and drizzle with the honey.

200 g (7 oz) goat's cheese, at room temperature

4 tablespoons milk

1 tablespoon sugar

20 medjool dates, pitted and scored down the centre

4 tablespoons pistachio nuts, lightly toasted and crushed

4 tablespoons honey

KEPOS STREET CHURROS

MAKES 24–30

Churros is a Kepos Street Kitchen signature dish. It's been on the menu since we opened in 2012 and I don't think our customers would let us take it off. This is a great dessert to serve for a group of people as the batter can be made in advance. Serve the churros immediately once they are cooked. We serve them in a paper bag with the cinnamon sugar. Our customers shake the bag around to coat the churros and there is nothing better than the smell of the warm churros and cinnamon.

Combine the buttermilk, butter, sugar, salt, vanilla seeds and 125 ml (4 fl oz/½ cup) of water in a saucepan. Bring to the boil over medium heat, then reduce the heat to low. Slowly add the flour, stirring with a wooden spoon until it has all been incorporated. Cook, stirring constantly, for a further 10 minutes. Remove from the heat and set aside to cool for 5 minutes.

Transfer the batter to an electric mixer with a paddle attachment and beat on medium speed for 2 minutes. Slowly add the eggs, one at a time, and beat until they are incorporated into the batter (you may need to reduce the mixer speed when adding the eggs). Increase the speed and beat for 2–3 minutes, until the batter is smooth and no longer sticks to the side of the bowl.

Spoon the batter into a piping (icing) bag with a star nozzle.

To make the cinnamon sugar, mix the sugar and cinnamon together in a bowl. Set aside.

Using a deep-fryer or a large deep saucepan, add the oil and heat to 170°C (340°F). If you don't have a thermometer, drop in a cube of bread—the oil is hot enough when the bread turns golden brown in 20 seconds. Pipe 10 cm (4 inch) lengths of the batter into the oil and cook in batches for 3–4 minutes, until golden. Remove the churros with a slotted spoon, drop them into the cinnamon sugar and turn to coat. Serve warm.

NOTE

The churros are lovely served with store-bought dulce de leche or caramel, with a sprinkle of sea salt flakes.

200 ml (7 fl oz) buttermilk

100 g (3½ oz) unsalted butter

1 tablespoon caster (superfine) sugar

½ teaspoon salt

seeds of 1 vanilla bean

300 g (10½ oz/2 cups) plain (all-purpose) flour, sifted

4 large eggs

vegetable oil or rice bran oil, for deep-frying

CINNAMON SUGAR

200 g (7 oz) caster (superfine) sugar

1 teaspoon ground cinnamon

PISTACHIO FRANGIPANE SLICE

MAKES 12–16 SLICES

Recipes should always be versatile and able to be adjusted to meet your needs. You can definitely switch the pistachio meal to almond meal for a classic frangipane, and you can top the slice with fresh seasonal fruit before you bake it.

Preheat the oven to 170°C (340°F).

Lightly grease a 20 x 30 cm (8 x 12 inch) baking tin and line with baking paper. Roll out the pastry on a lightly floured work surface to line the base of the tin. Press the pastry into the tin and bake for 10 minutes. Remove from the oven and cool to room temperature.

Combine the melted butter with the eggs in a bowl, then stir in the vanilla seeds and lemon zest. Set aside.

Put the pistachios in a food processor and chop until finely ground. Transfer to a bowl and mix in the icing sugar and 3 tablespoons flour. Tip onto the egg mixture and mix until combined.

Spread the pistachio mixture over the cooled pastry base and bake for 25–30 minutes, until firm to the touch.

1 quantity sweet shortcrust pastry (page 243)

3 tablespoons plain (all-purpose) flour, plus extra for dusting

250 g (9 oz) butter, melted and slightly cooled

4 eggs

seeds of 1 vanilla bean

grated zest of 1 lemon

250 g (9 oz/1⅔ cups) pistachio nuts

250 g (9 oz/2 cups) icing (confectioners') sugar

HONEY AND CRANBERRY CAKE

SERVES 8–10

Honey cakes remind me of September and October back home as that's when most cake shops would be serving several variations of this. Most of them would tend to be as simple as this one, but with a bit of creativity you can decorate even the simplest cake so that it looks amazing.

Preheat the oven to 170°C (340°F). Grease or oil a kugelhopf tin.

Sift the flour, sugar, baking powder, cinnamon and ginger into a bowl. Combine the honey, oil and eggs in a separate bowl and whisk together. Add the flour mixture and mix to combine.

Soak the cranberries in the boiling water for 1 minute, then tip into the batter and stir to combine.

Pour the batter into the prepared tin and bake for 40–45 minutes, until the cake is lightly golden. Cool the cake in the tin for 10 minutes, then turn out onto a wire rack to cool.

To make the glaze, combine the egg white, icing sugar and cinnamon in a small bowl. Working quickly, drizzle the glaze over the top of the cake before it sets, then scatter with the cranberries.

NOTE

You will need 1 egg to yield 1½ tablespoons of egg white. Separate the egg and set the yolk aside for another recipe. Lightly whisk the egg white. You should be able to measure out the 1½ tablespoons. If you use the whole egg white, it will be too much for the glaze.

300 g (10½ oz/2 cups) plain (all-purpose) flour

225 g (8 oz) caster (superfine) sugar

1½ tablespoons baking powder

1½ tablespoons ground cinnamon

1½ teaspoons ground ginger

375 g (13 oz) honey

180 ml (6 fl oz) vegetable oil

3 eggs

100 g (3½ oz) dried cranberries

180 ml (6 fl oz) boiling water

GLAZE

1½ tablespoons egg white (see Note)

120 g (4¼ oz) icing (confectioners') sugar, sifted

¼ teaspoon ground cinnamon

1½ tablespoons dried cranberries

NUTTY PIE

SERVES 8–10

Mum's favourite desserts usually contain nuts and this tart will definitely make her proud. It might even become her 'go to' recipe and could replace her own version. I'm not sure how likely that is, but I'm happy to give it a go!

Preheat the oven to 180°C (350°F). Spray a 24 cm (9½ inch) tart (flan) tin with non-stick oil spray.

Roll out the pastry on a lightly floured work surface to make a 30 cm (12 inch) round. Press the pastry into the base and side of the prepared tin. Set aside in the fridge while you prepare the filling.

Put the maple syrup, brown sugar and butter in a large saucepan and bring to the boil over medium heat. Remove the pan from the heat, add the rest of the ingredients and mix until well combined, working quickly to prevent the eggs from scrambling.

Pour the mixture into the pastry shell. Bake for 30–35 minutes, until the pie is firm to the touch and the pastry edges are golden. Serve the pie warm or cold.

1 quantity sweet shortcrust pastry (page 243)

plain (all-purpose) flour, for dusting

250 ml (9 fl oz/1 cup) pure maple syrup

120 g (4¼ oz) light brown sugar

100 g (3½ oz) butter

1 tablespoon coconut cream

100 g (3½ oz/1 cup) pecans

100 g (3½ oz) whole almonds

4 tablespoons hazelnuts, toasted and skinned

50 g (1¾ oz) caster (superfine) sugar

3 eggs, lightly whisked

FLOURLESS CHOCOLATE AND HALVA SWISS ROLL

SERVES 8–10

The combination of chocolate and halva works well as the halva adds a slightly savoury flavour and a nice crumbly texture.

Preheat the oven to 170°C (340°F). Lightly grease a 24 x 32 cm (9½ x 12¾ inch) Swiss roll (jelly roll) tin and line with baking paper. Spray the paper with non-stick oil spray and then sprinkle the paper with 3 tablespoons of the caster sugar.

Using an electric mixer with a whisk attachment, whisk the egg whites on high speed for 2–3 minutes, until soft peaks form. Gradually add the remaining 70 g (2½ oz) caster sugar and whisk for 4–5 minutes, until firm and glossy.

In a separate bowl, whisk the egg yolks with the vanilla seeds on high speed for 4–5 minutes, until the mixture is light, fluffy and increased in size. Gently fold in the egg white mixture while sifting in the cocoa powder. Pour into the prepared tin and bake for 15–20 minutes, until the sponge is cooked. Set aside to cool to room temperature.

While the cake is cooling, make the chocolate filling. Put the chocolate in a heatproof bowl over a saucepan of simmering water, making sure that the bowl does not touch the water. Stir until melted and smooth. Remove from the heat and set aside.

Whip the cream until soft peaks form. Set aside.

Whisk the egg yolks and sugar until pale and fluffy. Fold into the melted chocolate while the chocolate is still warm but not hot, then quickly and gently fold in the whipped cream so that the chocolate doesn't cool and crystallise.

Spread the chocolate filling over the cooled cake. Flake the halva over the top and roll up lengthways.

125 g (4½ oz) caster (superfine) sugar
3 large eggs, separated
seeds of 1 vanilla bean
2 tablespoons cocoa powder
150 g (5½ oz) halva, finely chopped

CHOCOLATE FILLING
350 g (12 oz) good-quality dark chocolate
500 ml (17 fl oz/2 cups) thin (pouring) cream
4 egg yolks
80 g (2¾ oz) caster (superfine) sugar

ORANGE AND HAZELNUT TEA CAKE

SERVES 8

Polenta cakes may sound complicated to make but they really are a simple gluten-free option. Most polenta recipes tend to use almond meal but I've used hazelnut meal as it gives the cake a much deeper colour and a nuttier flavour. It's lovely served with plain Greek-style yoghurt to balance the sweetness and richness of the orange syrup.

Preheat the oven to 160°C (320°F). Lightly grease a 24 cm (9½ inch) springform cake tin and line the base with baking paper.

Using an electric mixer with a paddle attachment, whisk the butter and 180 g (6 oz) of the sugar with the vanilla seeds and orange zest until light and fluffy, about 5 minutes. Add the eggs and whisk until combined.

While the mixer is running, combine the hazelnut meal, polenta and baking powder. Pour the mixture over the butter mixture and mix on low speed until combined.

Spoon the mixture into the prepared tin and bake for 40–45 minutes, until lightly golden and cooked through when tested with a skewer.

While the cake is cooking, prepare the garnish. Peel the oranges into large strips then slice the peel thinly. Place the sugar and water in a saucepan over low to medium heat and simmer until sugar has completely dissolved. Add the strips of orange peel and cook for 4–5 minutes until they have softened up.

Remove the saucepan from the heat and set aside until ready to use.

Cool the cake in the tin for at least 5 minutes before turning out onto a wire rack. Spoon the syrup and strips of peel over the cake. Finish with the toasted hazelnuts.

180 g (6 oz) butter, at room temperature

230 g (8 oz) caster (superfine) sugar

seeds of 1 vanilla bean

grated zest and juice of 2 oranges

3 large eggs

180 g (6 oz) hazelnut meal

100 g (3½ oz) instant polenta

1 teaspoon baking powder

GARNISH

2 oranges

110 g (3¾ oz/½ cup) caster (superfine) sugar

185 ml (6 fl oz/¾ cup) water

50 g (1¾ oz/⅓ cup) hazelnuts, lightly toasted

CHOCOLATE AND SALTED TAHINI BROWNIES

MAKES 12–16

Brownies are always delicious but the addition of the tahini and salt bring these to another level. If you don't want to use the tahini, you could replace it with dulce de leche or jam. If using jam, reduce the quantity by half, as the jam will not hold its form as well as the tahini or dulce de leche.

Preheat the oven to 170°C (340°F). Grease a 20 x 30 cm (8 x 12 inch) baking tin and line with baking paper.

Put the chocolate and butter in a heatproof bowl over a saucepan of simmering water, making sure the bowl does not touch the water. Melt until combined and smooth. Remove from the heat.

Using an electric mixer, whisk the eggs and sugar together until light and fluffy. Fold the flour into the chocolate mixture until combined and smooth, then fold the chocolate mixture into the egg mixture until combined. Pour the mixture into the prepared tin.

Mix the tahini and honey together in a small bowl to make a thick, gluggy mixture. Dollop spoonfuls of the tahini mixture on top of the chocolate mixture in the tin and use a spoon to swirl it through. Sprinkle the sea salt flakes over the batter. Bake for 25 minutes, or until the brownies are set but still moist and fudgy. Remove from the oven and leave to cool in the tin for 1 hour before cutting.

300 g (10½ oz) good-quality dark chocolate, chopped

250 g (9 oz) butter

5 large eggs

300 g (10½ oz) caster (superfine) sugar

160 g (5½ oz) plain (all-purpose) flour, sifted

110 g (3¾ oz) tahini

4 tablespoons honey

1 tablespoon sea salt flakes

PERSIAN LOVE CAKE

SERVES 8–10

The story goes that a young woman made this cake in order to make a prince fall in love with her. I don't know if her plan worked, or if this story is even true. But I do know that this has a great combination of Middle Eastern flavours and makes a beautiful, impressive dessert. It's a cake that's easy to fall in love with.

Preheat the oven to 180°C (350°F). Spray a 24 cm (9½ inch) springform cake tin with non-stick oil and line the base with baking paper.

Put the almond meal, hazelnut meal, sugars and butter in a large bowl. Using a wooden spoon, work the mixture together until combined and the sugar has dissolved. Add the eggs, pomegranate molasses, yoghurt, spices, rosewater and vanilla seeds and mix to combine.

Pour the batter into the prepared tin and smooth the top with a spatula or the back of a spoon. Bake for 55–60 minutes, until the cake is firm to the touch. Remove from the oven and leave in the tin to cool to room temperature.

Take the cooled cake out of the tin and garnish with the pistachios and barberries or cranberries.

150 g (5½ oz/1½ cups) almond meal

150 g (5½ oz) hazelnut meal

220 g (7¾ oz/1 cup) caster (superfine) sugar

220 g (7¾ oz) light brown sugar

125 g (4½ oz) butter, at room temperature

2 eggs, lightly beaten

2 tablespoons pomegranate molasses

250 g (9 oz) Greek-style yoghurt

1½ teaspoons freshly grated nutmeg

2 teaspoons ground cinnamon

½ teaspoon ground cardamom

1 tablespoon rosewater

seeds of 1 vanilla bean

100 g (3½ oz/⅔ cup) pistachio nuts, to garnish

50 g (1¾ oz) barberries or cranberries, to garnish

LAYERED TURKISH DELIGHT PAVLOVA

SERVES 8

I always struggle to find light desserts to serve at the end of a meal as most people tend to like chocolate-based desserts. The pink grapefruit in this pavlova has a lovely bitter flavour that cuts through the sweetness of the meringue and balances a rich meal. If you don't like the bitterness of the grapefruit it can be substituted with orange or any other citrus, but I suggest giving it a try as I think you'll be pleasantly surprised.

Preheat the oven to 160°C (320°F). Spray a 20 x 30 cm (8 x 12 inch) cake tin with non-stick oil and line with baking paper.

Using an electric mixer fitted with a whisk attachment, whisk the egg whites for 2–3 minutes, until soft peaks form. With the machine running, slowly add the caster sugar and then whisk for a further 8–10 minutes, until firm and glossy. Use a metal spoon to fold in the vinegar and rosewater.

Spoon the meringue mixture into the prepared tin and smooth the top. Bake for exactly 20 minutes, then remove from the oven and set aside to cool completely. Don't worry if the meringue looks a bit rustic when you take it out of the oven.

Put the mascarpone, cream and icing sugar in a large bowl and whisk until soft peaks form.

To assemble, cut the meringue in half so there are two 20 x 15 cm (8 x 6 inch) pieces. Put one piece on a serving plate and top with half the mascarpone mixture, half the grapefruit segments and half the Turkish delight. Top with the remaining meringue, then the remaining mascarpone mixture, grapefruit and Turkish delight. Scatter the pistachios and rose petals over the top.

7 egg whites, at room temperature

375 g (13 oz) caster (superfine) sugar

2 tablespoons white vinegar

1 tablespoon rosewater

250 g (9 oz) mascarpone cheese

250 ml (9 fl oz/1 cup) thin (pouring) cream

50 g (1¾ oz) icing (confectioners') sugar

4–5 pink grapefruit, segmented (see page 245)

300 g (10½ oz) good-quality Turkish delight, finely chopped

3 tablespoons pistachio nuts, lightly toasted and crushed

edible dried rose petals, to garnish

BANANA KATAIFI TARTE TATIN

SERVES 8–10

Tarte tatin is one of my favourite desserts. This one is a playful twist on the classic and the kataifi pastry gives it a crisper base. It's a fantastic dessert for entertaining as you can have most of the preparation done in advance and bake it when you're ready for dessert. It's delicious with vanilla or chocolate ice cream. You can change the fruit to apples, pears, peaches or apricots, or any other fruit that will hold its shape when cooked. You could also scatter crumbled pistachio nuts over the bananas to resemble a Greek kataifi dessert.

Preheat the oven to 170°C (340°F).

Heat a 24 cm (9½ inch) ovenproof frying pan over medium–low heat. Add the sugar and 50 ml (1½ fl oz) of water and cook, swirling the pan without stirring, for 7–8 minutes, until the caramel turns a nut-brown colour. Add the butter and stir to combine. Remove the pan from the heat and set aside.

Put the kataifi pastry in a large bowl and gently separate it with your hands. Pour in the melted butter and gently mix through.

Carefully arrange the banana pieces in the pan with the caramel. Spread the kataifi pastry over the top of the banana in an even layer. Press down and flatten the pastry, then bake for 20–25 minutes, until golden brown.

To serve, carefully turn the tarte tatin out onto a large plate.

220 g (7¾ oz/1 cup) caster (superfine) sugar

50 g (1¾ oz) butter

150 g (5½ oz) kataifi pastry

60 g (2¼ oz) butter, melted

6–8 bananas, cut into 3 cm (1¼ inch) pieces

APPLE, DATE AND HONEY CAKE

SERVES 8–10

My apple, date and honey cake requires minimal effort but has maximum impact. The apples can be replaced with pears, apricots, figs or poached quinces, and the dates can be swapped for any other dried fruit.

Preheat the oven to 170°C (340°F). Spray a 24 cm (9½ inch) springform cake tin with non-stick oil and line the base with baking paper. Spray the paper with oil.

To make the caramel apples, put the sugar and honey in a large frying pan. Cook over medium heat, stirring occasionally, until the mixture forms a golden caramel—this will take about 8–10 minutes. Add the butter and stir until melted. Add the apple wedges and cook for 5–8 minutes, until the apples are golden and the sugar syrup is sticky. Stir the apples only once or twice during cooking so they don't break up. Remove from the heat and set aside to cool to room temperature.

Heat the butter in a separate frying pan over medium heat and cook for 10–12 minutes, until melted and golden brown. Remove from the heat and set aside.

Put the almond meal, flour and dates in a bowl. Stir until the dates have separated and are evenly coated in the almond meal and flour.

Using an electric mixer fitted with a whisk attachment, whisk the egg whites until soft peaks form. Gradually add the sugar and whisk until medium peaks form, about 5 minutes.

Gently pour the browned butter over the date mixture and stir to combine, then fold in the egg white mixture.

Pour the batter into the prepared tin. Arrange the cooked apple wedges on top, trying not to add any excess liquid (reserve the liquid to drizzle over the cooked cake). Scatter the flaked almonds over the apple and bake for 30–35 minutes, until the cake is golden and cooked through. Remove from the oven and cool in the tin for 20 minutes.

Drizzle the honey or reserved caramel over the cake and serve warm or at room temperature.

NOTES

You can use the leftover liquid from the caramel apples to drizzle over the cooked cake instead of using honey.

You can also make this into a slice by cooking it in a 20 x 30 cm (8 x 12 inch) cake tin.

200 g (7 oz) butter

120 g (4¼ oz) almond meal

80 g (2¾ oz) plain (all-purpose) flour, sifted

10 dried dates, pitted and coarsely chopped

6 egg whites

220 g (7 oz/1 cup) caster (superfine) sugar

30 g (1 oz) flaked almonds

4 tablespoons honey (optional, see Notes)

CARAMEL APPLES

60 g (2¼ oz) caster (superfine) sugar

2 tablespoons honey

30 g (1 oz) butter, cubed

3 large red apples, peeled, cored and cut into 8 wedges

JAFFA TEA CAKE WITH MARZIPAN

SERVES 8–10

Jaffa, Tel Aviv, is my home town and growing up we always took pride in the knowledge that some of the best oranges in the world come from there. Chocolate and orange are a match made in heaven, and adding a little marzipan gives this cake a lovely bitter almond flavour. You can substitute any dried fruit you like for the marzipan. Halva is also a lovely substitute.

Preheat the oven to 160°C (320°F). Spray a 24 cm (9½ inch) springform cake tin with non-stick oil and line with baking paper.

Using an electric mixer, beat the butter and sugar until light and fluffy. Add the orange zest and one of the eggs and mix well. Add the remaining eggs, one at a time.

Sift the flour, cocoa, baking powder, bicarbonate of soda and salt into a bowl. Toss the chocolate and marzipan pieces through the dry ingredients. Fold the dry ingredients into the butter and sugar mixture until combined.

Spoon the batter into the prepared tin and smooth the surface. Bake the cake for 50 minutes, or until cooked through and golden. Remove from the oven and set aside for 5 minutes before turning out onto a wire rack to cool.

To make the icing, mix the icing sugar, orange zest and orange juice together in a bowl until smooth.

Drizzle the icing over the cool cake.

225 g (8 oz) butter, at room temperature

240 g (8½ oz) caster (superfine) sugar

grated zest of 1 orange

5 eggs

225 g (8 oz/1½ cups) plain (all-purpose) flour

4 tablespoons cocoa powder

1½ teaspoons baking powder

1½ teaspoons bicarbonate of soda (baking soda)

¾ teaspoon salt

300 g (10½ oz) good-quality dark chocolate, cut into coarse shards

300 g (10½ oz) marzipan, chopped

ORANGE DRIZZLE ICING

100 g (3½ oz) icing (confectioners') sugar, sifted

grated zest of 1 orange

3 tablespoons orange juice

HAZELNUT, DATE AND RICOTTA CAKE

SERVES 8–10

If you are tired of traditional Christmas cake, give this one a try.
It's a good gluten-free option for a dessert or cake any time.

Preheat the oven to 170°C (340°F). Grease a 24 cm (9½ inch) springform cake tin and line the base with baking paper.

Using an electric mixer, beat the butter and sugar until light and fluffy. Add the eggs, one at a time, mixing well after each addition. Add the ricotta and beat until fluffy and creamy. Fold in the dates, hazelnuts and almond meal.

Pour the batter into the prepared tin and bake for 40–45 minutes, until the cake is golden brown and firm to the touch. Remove from the oven and set aside to cool completely in the tin for at least 1 hour.

To make the topping, put the ricotta, icing sugar and vanilla seeds in a bowl and mix to combine.

Spread the topping over the cooled cake and scatter the dates and hazelnuts over the top.

250 g (9 oz) butter, at room temperature

250 g (9 oz) caster (superfine) sugar

4 eggs

150 g (5½ oz) firm ricotta cheese

300 g (10½ oz) dried dates, pitted and coarsely chopped

150 g (5½ oz) hazelnuts, toasted, skinned and coarsely crushed

75 g (2½ oz) almond meal

TOPPING

200 g (7 oz) firm ricotta cheese

100 g (3½ oz) icing (confectioners') sugar, sifted

seeds of 1 vanilla bean

10 dried dates, pitted and coarsely chopped

70 g (2½ oz) hazelnuts, toasted, skinned and coarsely chopped

CANDIED SESAME
SEED BARS

MAKES 12

As a youngster, I used to walk to school and on the way I'd pass street stalls that sold sesame bars, coconut bars and freshly baked doughnuts. Nothing says childhood more to me than sesame bars.

Lightly toast the sesame seeds in a shallow frying pan over medium-low heat, tossing regularly and watching carefully to make sure they don't burn. Once the sesame seeds turn golden, tip them into a bowl and set aside.

Combine the sugar, honey and 2 tablespoons of water in a saucepan. Bring to the boil over medium–high heat and cook for 5 minutes, or until caramelised and a light golden colour. Add the sesame seeds and mix to combine.

Pour the sesame mixture onto a 30 cm (12 inch) sheet of greaseproof paper. Top with another sheet of greaseproof paper and gently roll over the top with a rolling pin until the mixture is smooth and about 2 cm (¾ inch) thick. Allow to set for 15–20 minutes—the mixture will be firm to the touch but still pliable. Remove the top layer of paper and cut the mixture into 12 bars.

Store the sesame bars in an airtight container for up to 3 weeks.

NOTE

Roll out the sesame mixture until it reaches your preferred thickness, then cut the bars to whatever size you like.

290 g (10¼ oz/2 cups) sesame seeds
220 g (7 oz/1 cup) caster (superfine) sugar
150 g (5½ oz) honey

PISTACHIO AND ROSEWATER CAKE WITH PLUMS AND MASCARPONE

SERVES 8–10

This light and nutty cake will become your new favourite sponge recipe. You can change the nuts and fruit to whatever flavours you like and you can add any other flavouring. For example, substitute almonds for the pistachio nuts and almond extract for the rosewater, or use other nuts and vanilla bean paste. I just love the combination of pistachios, plums and rosewater.

Preheat the oven to 160°C (320°F). Grease a 24 cm (9½ inch) springform cake tin and line the base with baking paper. Line a roasting tin with baking paper.

Lightly toast the pistachios in a frying pan over medium heat. Allow to cool, then coarsely chop the nuts until they are about the size of rock salt granules.

Using an electric mixer fitted with a whisk attachment, whisk the egg whites until firm peaks form. Transfer to another bowl.

Add the egg yolks and 200 g (7 oz) of the caster sugar to the mixer bowl (there's no need to clean it) and whisk until fluffy and creamy. Fold in half the chopped pistachios, then fold in the egg whites, the remaining pistachios, lemon zest and rosewater. Don't overfold the mixture as you want to keep it as aerated as possible.

Pour into the prepared cake tin and bake for 30–35 minutes, until the cake is lightly firm to the touch but cooked through. Remove from the oven and set aside to cool in the tin.

Increase the oven temperature to 180°C (350°F). Put the plum halves in the prepared roasting tin and sprinkle with the remaining caster sugar and squeeze over the lemon juice. Roast for 10–12 minutes, until slightly tender.

Just before serving, whisk the mascarpone, cream and icing sugar until soft peaks form.

Remove the cake from the tin and spread the mascarpone cream over the top. Add the plums and drizzle with the cooking juices.

220 g (7 oz) pistachio nuts
5 large eggs, separated
300 g (10½ oz) caster (superfine) sugar
grated zest of 1 lemon
1 teaspoon rosewater
6 plums, halved, stones removed
½ lemon
250 g (9 oz) mascarpone cheese
300 ml (10½ fl oz) thin (pouring) cream
2 tablespoons icing (confectioners') sugar

FLOURLESS CHOCOLATE AND ALMOND MUD CAKE

SERVES 8–10

I enjoy baking flourless cakes and desserts. This one is a great addition to your repertoire as it's quite simple to make. It's very moist and will keep for several days. If you want to make it even richer, try topping the cake with a chocolate ganache (see Note).

Preheat the oven to 170°C (340°F). Spray a 24 cm (9½ inch) springform cake tin with non-stick oil and line the base with baking paper.

Put a heatproof bowl over a saucepan of simmering water, making sure that the bowl does not touch the water. Add the chocolate and melt until smooth.

Transfer the chocolate to a food processor and add the butter, sugar, almond meal and eggs. Blitz to combine, then scrape down the side of the bowl and blitz again.

Pour the batter into the prepared tin. Bake for 30–35 minutes, until the cake is firm on the top but still moist inside. Remove from the oven and set aside to cool in the tin.

Serve the cooled cake dusted with cocoa powder.

NOTE

To make a chocolate ganache, melt 200 g (7 oz) dark chocolate with 200 ml (7 fl oz) thin (pouring) cream. Cool to room temperature, then spread the ganache over the cooled cake.

250 g (9 oz) good-quality dark cooking chocolate, chopped

150 g (5½ oz) butter, at room temperature

250 g (9 oz) caster (superfine) sugar

200 g (7 oz/2 cups) almond meal

6 eggs

good-quality cocoa powder, for dusting

HOT JAM DOUGHNUTS

MAKES 24 MINI DOUGHNUTS

Who can resist the smell of freshly cooked doughnuts? These are so easy to make—don't be put off by the yeast. We like raspberry jam in our house, but you can change it to any flavour you like.

Combine the milk and butter in a saucepan and warm over medium-low heat. When the butter is melted, remove the pan from the heat.

Combine the flour, sugar, yeast and salt in a bowl. Beat the eggs into the warmed milk, then pour into the dry ingredients. Using an electric mixer fitted with a dough hook (or your hands), knead the dough until smooth and silky (about 10 minutes by hand). Put the dough in a bowl, cover with a damp tea towel (dish towel) and leave to rise in a warm place until the dough has doubled in size, about 45 minutes to 1 hour.

Punch down the dough and knead again until smooth. Cut the dough in half and roll each half into a 25 cm (10 inch) log. Cut each log into 12 pieces, roll each into a rough ball and place on a tray lined with baking paper. Cover loosely and leave to rise for 15 minutes.

Using a deep-fryer or a large deep saucepan, heat the oil to 170°C (340°F). If you don't have a thermometer, drop in a cube of bread—the oil is hot enough when the bread turns golden brown in 20 seconds. Cook the doughnuts, a few at a time, for 5 minutes each batch, turning them halfway through cooking so they brown evenly. Remove and drain on paper towel, then roll in the extra sugar to coat.

Spoon the jam into a piping (icing) bag fitted with a small nozzle and pipe into the centre of each doughnut. Serve warm.

125 ml (4 fl oz/½ cup) milk

15 g (½ oz) unsalted butter

250 g (9 oz/1⅔ cups) strong flour

25 g (¾ oz) caster (superfine) sugar, plus extra for rolling

1½ teaspoons instant dried yeast

¼ teaspoon salt

2 eggs

2 litres (70 fl oz/8 cups) rice bran oil, for deep-frying

raspberry jam, to fill the doughnuts

SEMOLINA AND COCONUT CAKE WITH LEMON SYRUP

MAKES 12–16 SLICES

Basbousa is a syrup cake that brings back a lot of childhood memories—not that I was a big fan of it when I was younger. All children know that chocolate cake is the best cake, and what child would want to eat a syrup cake? This was one of my mum's favourite cakes, so she made it fairly regularly and, while it wasn't a favourite of mine then, now that I'm an adult and live far away from my mum, I love the crumbly, syrupy texture. This version is my interpretation of the classic recipe.

Preheat the oven to 180°C (350°F). Grease a 24 cm (9½ inch) springform cake tin and line it with baking paper.

In a large bowl, mix the semolina, sugar, desiccated coconut, milk and melted butter until combined.

Pour the batter into the prepared tin. Bake for 30–35 minutes, or until the cake is cooked through and golden.

While the cake is baking, make the syrup. Put the sugar and water in a small saucepan and bring to the boil. Boil for 2–3 minutes, stirring occasionally, until the sugar has dissolved. Cook for a further 5 minutes, then add the lemon juice. Bring to the boil then remove from the heat and set aside.

When ready, remove the cooked cake from the oven and immediately pour the syrup over the top—it will soak through the cake but it may take about 10 minutes for all the syrup to soak in. Sprinkle over the toasted coconut flakes, then serve at room temperature.

400 g (14 oz) fine semolina
200 g (7 oz) caster (superfine) sugar
200 g (7 oz) desiccated coconut
300 ml (10½ fl oz) milk
200 g (7 oz) butter, melted
50 g (1¾ oz) flaked coconut, lightly toasted

LEMON SYRUP
300 g (10½ oz) sugar
300 ml (10½ fl oz) water
1 tablespoon of lemon juice

APRICOT, HONEY AND NUT SLICE

SERVES 8–10

This cake-like slice is great served as a dessert or with a cup of mint tea. If I'm serving it warm, I like to add a scoop of vanilla ice cream, but it's equally delicious at room temperature.

Preheat the oven to 170°C (340°F). Grease a 20 x 30 cm (8 x 12 inch) cake tin, line with baking paper and spray with non-stick oil.

Mix the semolina, flour and baking powder in a large bowl.

Whisk the apple juice, melted butter, eggs and vanilla seeds in a separate bowl until combined. Pour into the dry ingredients and mix until combined.

Pour the mixture into the prepared tin and scatter the apricots, hazelnuts and almonds over the top. Bake for 35–40 minutes, until the slice is cooked through and lightly golden brown.

While the slice is baking, put the honey and 125 ml (4 fl oz/½ cup) of water in a saucepan and bring to the boil over medium heat, then remove the pan from the heat.

Remove the cooked slice from the oven and set aside to cool for 5 minutes. Use a pastry brush to glaze the slice with the syrup.

600 g (1 lb 5 oz) semolina

200 g (7 oz/1⅓ cups) plain (all-purpose) flour

1 teaspoon baking powder

300 ml (10½ fl oz) apple juice

160 g (5½ oz) butter, melted and cooled

6 eggs

seeds of 1 vanilla bean

150 g (5½ oz) dried apricots, coarsely chopped

150 g (5½ oz) hazelnuts, coarsely chopped

150 g (5½ oz) almonds, coarsely chopped

150 g (5½ oz) honey

LABNEH AND HONEY ICE CREAM

MAKES 1 LITRE (35 FL OZ/4 CUPS)

I'd like to take credit for this recipe, but it comes from our friends at Booza Ice Cream, a boutique ice-cream producer in Sydney. They create amazing and delicious Middle Eastern inspired flavours. Thank you, Booza Ice Cream.

Pour the milk and cream into a saucepan and stir to combine. Heat over low heat until almost boiling, then remove from the heat.

Whisk the sugar and honey into the milk mixture until dissolved. Pour into a heatproof bowl, then place the bowl inside a larger bowl of ice to cool. Transfer to the fridge to cool for at least 2 hours.

Stir the labneh through the chilled ice cream mixture, then pour into an ice-cream maker and churn according to the manufacturer's directions.

500 ml (17 fl oz/2 cups) milk

150 ml (5 fl oz) thin (pouring) cream

175 g (6 oz) raw (demerara) sugar

45 g (1½ oz) honey

100 g (3½ oz) labneh

YOGHURT, LEMON AND BERRY PANNA COTTA

MAKES 12 SMALL JARS

I find panna cotta is a delicious dessert to serve at the end of a meal. It can be made in advance. This version has a light refreshing flavour and the yoghurt adds a touch of acidity.

Put the gelatine sheets in a bowl of icy-cold water. Set aside to soften.

Lightly whisk the yoghurt and lemon zest in a bowl. Set aside.

Combine the milk, cream, caster sugar and vanilla seeds in a large saucepan. Heat over medium heat until almost boiling, then remove from the heat and leave to cool for about 4 minutes.

Drain the gelatine sheets, add to the hot milk mixture and whisk until dissolved. Add the yoghurt mixture and stir until smooth and creamy. Strain the mixture into a bowl with a lip and pour into 12 jars or small ramekins, leaving room to add the berries when serving. Place in the fridge to set for at least 4 hours, preferably overnight.

To serve, mix the berries with the icing sugar. Spoon the berries over the set panna cotta and sprinkle with the pistachios.

4 gelatine sheets

400 g (14 oz) plain yoghurt

grated zest of 1 lemon

300 ml (10½ fl oz) milk

350 ml (12 fl oz) thin (pouring) cream

160 g (5½ oz) caster (superfine) sugar

seeds of 1 vanilla bean

500 g (1 lb 2 oz) mixed berries

1 tablespoon icing (confectioners') sugar

4 tablespoons pistachio nuts, coarsely chopped

CHAPTER SEVEN

DIPS, SPREADS & RUBS

The world of Middle Eastern dips extends far beyond hummus, although that is definitely the one that's probably best known and loved outside the region. The good news is that if you like hummus, you'll probably like lots of these dips, too. They're all delicious and different in flavour, but they're also very easy to make. They can be smoky, spicy, garlicky or lemony. We've included our favourite version of hummus, which you'll find on our table most evenings, and also a recipe for pumpkin hummus, a variation on the classic. There are several other dips to expand your repertoire, and all of these will be great additions to any shared table. Rubs and marinades are such an easy way to flavour meat or vegetables. Use the bastourma rub on fish, add some chermoula to chicken breasts before barbecuing or sprinkle hazelnut dukkah on your salads to give them another dimension.

HUMMUS

MAKES ABOUT 1 KG (2 LB 4 OZ)

There are many different ways of making hummus and everyone thinks their version is best. You can use tinned chickpeas but the result will not be as silky and smooth. If you are using tinned chickpeas, you will need 500 g (1 lb 2 oz) drained chickpeas. Bring them to the boil, add the baking powder and cook for a further 5 minutes.

150 g (5½ oz) dried chickpeas
¼ teaspoon baking powder
5 garlic cloves
400 g (14 oz) raw tahini
1 teaspoon salt
pinch of ground cumin
100 ml (3½ fl oz) lemon juice

In a large saucepan or bowl, soak the chickpeas in plenty of cold water (at least four times the quantity of the dried chickpeas) for at least 12 hours—overnight is good. Change the water at least twice during this time.

Drain the chickpeas and rinse well. Transfer to a large saucepan and cover with at least double the quantity of water to the chickpeas. Bring to the boil, then cover and cook over medium heat for 2 hours, topping up the water as necessary.

After 2 hours, if the chickpeas are soft, add the baking powder. (If not, continue cooking until they soften.) Cook for a further hour, or until the chickpeas start to break down but are not mushy.

Meanwhile, put the peeled whole garlic cloves in a food processor (don't use a stick blender) with 200 ml (7 fl oz) of water and blend until very smooth. Tip into a sieve and keep the liquid, discarding the puréed garlic.

Drain the chickpeas. Put them in the food processor and blend to a smooth paste; this will take 7–10 minutes. Add the tahini, reserved garlic water, salt and cumin. Blend well, scraping down the side occasionally and adding more water if necessary. Transfer to a large bowl. Gently whisk in the lemon juice (you don't want to over-aerate the hummus and lose the dense consistency).

Store the hummus in a sealed container in the fridge for up to 5 days.

PUMPKIN HUMMUS

MAKES ABOUT 800 G (1 LB 12 OZ)

Pumpkin hummus is a great take on the classic—it's easier to make and takes much less time and effort. Serve it as a dip when your guests arrive or as part of a shared table. It works equally well with fish and meat dishes.

700 g (1 lb 9 oz) butternut pumpkin (squash), peeled and cut into chunks
3 tablespoons olive oil
3 garlic cloves
white pepper, to season
200 g (7 oz) tahini
juice of 1–1½ lemons

Preheat the oven to 170°C (340°F). Line a baking tray with baking paper.

Put the pumpkin in a large bowl and toss with the olive oil and garlic cloves. Season with salt and white pepper. Spread over the baking tray and bake for 25–30 minutes, until the pumpkin is soft but not coloured.

When the pumpkin is cool enough to handle, transfer it to a food processor. Add 125 ml (4 fl oz/½ cup) of water and the tahini and lemon juice, to taste. Blitz until the mixture is smooth and well combined. Check the seasoning and add more salt and lemon juice, if needed.

Store the pumpkin hummus in a sealed container in the fridge for up to 5 days.

Pictured on page 209

MUHAMARA DIP

MAKES ABOUT 500 ML (17 FL OZ/2 CUPS)

We can all become bored with serving the same dishes, so it's great to add another dip to your repertoire. This dip also makes a lovely relish on sandwiches as it works well with most roasted meats.

4 red capsicums (peppers)

4 garlic cloves

60 g (2¼ oz) walnuts

60 g (2¼ oz) dry breadcrumbs

2 large fresh red chillies

3 tablespoons olive oil

3 tablespoons pomegranate molasses

juice of ½ lemon

1 teaspoon ground cumin

1 teaspoon ground coriander

1 teaspoon salt

Preheat the oven to 180°C (350°F).

Put the capsicums on a baking tray and roast for about 25–30 minutes, until they are quite coloured and almost charred. Using tongs, transfer the capsicums to a plastic bag. Wrap the plastic bag in a tea towel (dish towel) and set aside to cool for about 20 minutes.

When the capsicums are cool enough to handle, remove and discard the skin and seeds. Put the capsicum flesh, garlic, walnuts, breadcrumbs and red chillies in a food processor and blitz until the mixture forms a relatively smooth paste. Add the remaining ingredients and blitz until combined. Taste and season with a little more salt, if needed.

Store the dip in a sealed container in the fridge for up to 5 days.

Pictured on page 208

BABA GHANOUSH

MAKES ABOUT 300 ML (10½ FL OZ)

Baba ghanoush translates from Arabic as 'pampered poppa' or, as I say, 'spoiling dad'. It's my understanding that barbecuing is a male's job in most Mediterranean cultures. That's as much cooking as you would see most men doing! The name 'baba ghanoush' probably came from the fact that the men would chargrill the eggplants while barbecuing, and this dip would be more of a treat as they wouldn't often light the charcoal.

2 eggplants (aubergines)

2 tomatoes, chopped

2 handfuls coriander (cilantro), leaves picked and chopped

1 handful flat-leaf (Italian) parsley, leaves picked and chopped

3 spring onions (scallions), white part and some of the green part, finely chopped

3 garlic cloves, crushed

juice of 2 lemons

3 tablespoons olive oil

Heat the barbecue to high and put on the eggplants. Cook, turning, until the skins blister and burn and the centres are soft. Alternatively, place the eggplants on a naked flame on a gas cooktop and cook, turning with tongs, until blackened. Set aside to cool.

When the eggplants are cool enough to handle, peel off and discard the skin. Don't worry if there is still some black on the eggplant itself as that adds to the flavour. Finely chop the flesh and put it in a bowl.

Add the remaining ingredients to the chopped eggplant and mix until combined. Season with salt and freshly ground black pepper.

Store the dip in a sealed container in the fridge for up to 5 days.

Pictured on page 208

MUTABAL

MAKES ABOUT 300 ML (10½ FL OZ)

To me, the difference between mutabal and baba ghanoush is that mutabal contains only eggplant and tahini, while baba ghanoush has different variations and ingredients such as tomatoes, onions and herbs, and it doesn't necessarily contain tahini. Ordinarily, I don't like smoky flavours but I am drawn to this dish because the tahini gives it a nutty, creamy and delicate flavour and texture. It's great as a dip with drinks, as a condiment with meats or as part of a shared table. You can serve it drizzled with olive oil and sprinkled with pomegranate seeds and chopped herbs.

Heat the barbecue to high and put on the eggplants. Cook, turning, until the skins blister and burn. Alternatively, place the eggplants on a naked flame on a gas cooktop and cook, turning with tongs, until blackened. Set aside to cool.

When the eggplants are cool enough to handle, peel off and discard the skin. Put the eggplant flesh and garlic in a food processor and blitz until just combined. Add the tahini and lemon juice and blitz again, then season with salt.

Store the dip in a sealed container in the fridge for up to 5 days.

3 large eggplants (aubergines)
3 garlic cloves, crushed
120 g (4¼ oz) tahini
juice of 1 lemon

NOTES

Charring the eggplants on a barbecue or gas cooktop gives them a lovely smoky flavour. You can bake them in the oven, but they won't have the same flavour. Preheat the oven to 220°C (425°F) and cook the eggplants on a baking tray until charred.

If you are in a hurry, you can drop the charred eggplants into iced water to cool them down.

WHITE BEAN DIP

SERVES 6

This white bean dip is a play on a dish called musabaha, which is a chunkier hummus with a spicy, lemony flavour. The dip doesn't necessarily need the tahini, but it gives it a creamier texture and Mediterranean flavour. You can add more or less garlic and chilli for the garnish, depending on your taste.

Soak the beans in cold water for at least 8 hours, preferably overnight.

Drain and rinse the soaked beans well and put them in a large saucepan with plenty of fresh water. Cook over medium–low heat for 1½ hours, stirring occasionally and skimming from time to time. The beans will be soft but not too mushy. Add the bicarbonate of soda and cook for another 15–20 minutes, until the beans are very soft and have almost broken down. Drain the beans.

Set aside one-third of the beans. Put the remaining beans in a food processor with the garlic. Blitz to a smooth paste, then add the tahini, lemon juice and salt. Blitz again until combined.

To make the garnish, combine the garlic, chilli and lemon juice in a small bowl.

To serve, spoon the dip into a serving bowl and fold in the reserved beans. Sprinkle with the garnish and drizzle with olive oil.

Store the dip in a sealed container in the fridge for up to 5 days.

300 g (10½ oz/1½ cups) dried white beans
1 teaspoon bicarbonate of soda (baking soda)
1 garlic clove, crushed
100 g (3½ oz) tahini
juice of 1 lemon
1 teaspoon salt
olive oil, for drizzling

GARNISH
1–2 garlic cloves, crushed
1–2 small fresh green chillies, finely chopped
juice of 1 lemon

SHANKLISH CHEESE WITH ZA'ATAR

MAKES 20 SMALL BALLS

These versatile yoghurt cheese balls make a great snack or an accompaniment to a shared table. They can also be used to make a salad by flaking the balls and mixing them with fresh tomatoes and olive oil, or you could use them in a pasta dish.

Put the yoghurt and 200 ml (7 fl oz) of water in a saucepan and whisk to combine. Bring to a gentle simmer over medium–low heat, mixing once or twice until the mixture separates into curds and whey.

Line a colander with a large piece of muslin (cheesecloth) and pour in the yoghurt mixture. Drain over the sink until the mixture is firm, dry and cool. This will take about 2 hours.

Meanwhile, combine the remaining ingredients in a shallow bowl.

Transfer the firm yoghurt to a bowl. Season with salt and gently mix to combine. Using clean hands, shape the mixture into 20 even balls, then roll them in the za'atar mixture.

Traditionally these are kept in an airtight glass jar and covered completely with olive oil. They will keep like this in the fridge for around 2–3 months, but you can also store them in an airtight container in the fridge for up to 3 weeks.

1 kg (2 lb 4 oz) Greek-style yoghurt

1 tablespoon sweet paprika

1 small fresh red chilli, chopped and crushed

100 g (3½ oz) za'atar spice mix

NOTE

Za'atar spice mix, available in Middle Eastern grocery stores, contains dried za'atar leaves, sesame seeds, ground sumac and other spices.

TARAMASALATA

MAKES 500 ML (17 FL OZ/2 CUPS)

You can never have enough 'on arrival' dishes in your repertoire, and guests are always impressed by homemade taramasalata. You can also make this just to spoil yourself at home.

Rinse the bread slices under running water for just a few seconds. Firmly squeeze out the excess water.

Put the bread in a food processor with the fish roe, garlic and shallot and blend to a very fine paste. Add the lemon juice and then, with the motor running, slowly pour in the olive oil. The mixture will thicken. Season with salt and white pepper.

Store the dip in a sealed container in the fridge for up to 5 days.

Pictured opposite

4 slices white bread, crusts removed

100 g (3½ oz) fish roe (red lumpfish caviar, trout roe, salmon roe or cod roe)

1 garlic clove, crushed

2 French shallots, finely chopped

juice of ½ lemon

250 ml (9 fl oz/1 cup) light olive oil

white pepper, to season

TARATOR

MAKES ABOUT 250 ML (9 FL OZ/1 CUP)

Tarator is a versatile dip originating in Macedonia, Turkey or Bulgaria. It can also be served as a condiment with grilled fish. There are plenty of versions of tarator. I prefer using yoghurt instead of tahini because it gives a lighter, more refreshing taste. The nuts add a lovely complexity of flavour.

Lightly crush the pine nuts using a mortar and pestle. Transfer to a bowl. Crush the walnuts using the mortar and pestle. Tip the walnuts into the bowl with the pine nuts.

Add the yoghurt, olive oil, garlic and dill. Mix to combine, then season with sea salt.

NOTE

Tarator is best served on the day it is made. It can be stored in the fridge for up to 5 days, but the nuts might become a little soft.

Pictured on page 208

2 tablespoons pine nuts, lightly toasted

60 g (2¼ oz) walnuts, lightly toasted

150 g (5½ oz) Greek-style yoghurt

3 tablespoons olive oil

3 garlic cloves, crushed

1 tablespoon finely chopped dill

sea salt flakes, to season

FILFEL CHUMA

MAKES 600 G (1 LB 5 OZ)

I have always thought of filfel chuma as another form of harissa. It comes from Libya and is a relatively unknown condiment, with practically endless uses. It makes a fantastic marinade and can also be served with a grilled steak or used to season fish or other barbecued dishes. I also like to fry an egg with a tablespoon of filfel chuma and some olive oil for a spicy start to the day.

200 g (7 oz) sweet paprika
1 large fresh red chilli, finely chopped
2 fresh red bird's eye chillies, finely chopped
8 garlic cloves
1½ teaspoons salt
1 teaspoon caraway seeds, toasted and ground to a powder
200 ml (7 fl oz) light olive oil

Add all the ingredients except the olive oil to a food processor. Blitz until the mixture is combined but still chunky and coarse. Scrape down the side of the bowl. Add the oil and blitz again (don't overdo it as it should be oily and coarsely chopped).

Spoon the filfel chuma into a sterilised jar and store in the fridge for up to 3 weeks.

Pictured on page 222

CLASSIC HARISSA

MAKES APPROXIMATELY 800 G (1 LB 12 OZ)

Harissa recipes vary from one region to another in North Africa and the Middle East. This classic recipe was given to me by a friend who had retrieved it from his grandmother's recipe collection. I like this version because the spices are well balanced and it preserves well in the fridge.

200 g (7 oz) dried paprika chillies
10 large fresh red chillies, coarsely chopped
8 garlic cloves, crushed
2 teaspoons ground cumin
1 teaspoon ground coriander
100 ml (3½ fl oz) red wine vinegar or lemon juice (see Note)
350 ml (12 fl oz) light olive oil

Soak the paprika chillies in warm water for 2 hours. Drain and remove the stalks.

Add the soaked chillies, fresh chillies and garlic to a food processor and blend to a paste. Add the spices and vinegar or lemon juice and blend for 1 minute. Stir in the olive oil with a large spoon.

Spoon the harissa into a sterilised jar and store in the fridge for up to 3 weeks.

NOTE

If you are serving the harissa with meat, use the red wine vinegar; if you are using it with fish, use the lemon juice.

Pictured on page 222

GREEK-STYLE MARINADE

SUITABLE FOR A 1.5–2 KG (3 LB 5 OZ–4 LB 8 OZ) PIECE OF MEAT

This marinade goes really well with lamb but it can be used for any shish kebab on skewers. Marinate the meat pieces in the fridge for 3–4 hours before threading them onto the skewers. Alternatively, if you are marinating a whole piece of meat, marinate it for at least 3–4 hours, but preferably overnight.

---

2 brown onions

2 tomatoes

150 ml (5 fl oz) olive oil

juice of 1 small lemon

4 bay leaves

2 tablespoons dried oregano

Grate the onions, retaining the flesh and juice.

Crush the tomatoes in a food processor. Add the grated onion flesh and juice along with the remaining ingredients. Season with salt and freshly ground black pepper and blitz until smooth.

Store the marinade in a sealed container in the fridge for up to 5 days.

YOGHURT MARINADE

SUITABLE FOR A 1–1.5 KG (2 LB 4 OZ–3 LB 5 OZ) PIECE OF MEAT

Rub the marinade over lamb or chicken and marinate it in the fridge for at least 3–4 hours before cooking, but preferably leave it to marinate overnight. Lightly scrape off any excess marinade before cooking.

---

1 brown onion

300 g (10½ oz) Greek-style yoghurt

2 garlic cloves

1 tablespoon dried mint

Grate the onion, retaining the flesh and juice. Place in a bowl and add the yoghurt, garlic and mint. Season with salt and freshly ground black pepper and mix well.

Store the marinade in a sealed container in the fridge for up to 5 days.

Pictured on page 222

⑤

HARISSA DRESSING

MAKES ABOUT 1 LITRE (35 FL OZ/4 CUPS)

This is more of a vinegary style of harissa than the traditional harissa paste. It works much better if you are using it as a dressing rather than cooking with it. You can make harissa paste from this recipe by using less oil and vinegar and adding more chilli.

---

700 g (1 lb 9 oz) capsicums (peppers)

6 garlic cloves

2 large fresh green chillies

2 handfuls coriander (cilantro), coarsely chopped

1½ tablespoons mild paprika

1 tablespoon ground cumin

1 tablespoon ground coriander

2 tablespoons caster (superfine) sugar

50 ml (1½ fl oz) red wine vinegar

200 ml (7 fl oz) extra virgin olive oil

Preheat the oven to 180°C (350°F).

Put the capsicums on a baking tray and roast for about 25–30 minutes, until they are quite coloured and almost charred. Using tongs, transfer the capsicums to a plastic bag. Wrap the plastic bag in a tea towel (dish towel) and set aside to cool for about 20 minutes.

When the capsicums are cool enough to handle, remove and discard the skin and seeds. Put the flesh in a food processor along with the garlic, chillies and chopped coriander and blend to a paste. Add the spices and sugar and blend for 1 minute. Pour in the red wine vinegar and season with salt. With the motor running, slowly drizzle the olive oil into the dressing and blend until combined.

Store the dressing in a sealed container in the fridge for up to 2 weeks.

Pictured on page 223

ALL-PURPOSE SPICE BLEND

FILLS A 250 ML (9 FL OZ/1 CUP) JAR

This spice blend is based on the traditional Lebanese spice blend, baharat, which translates as 'a blend of spices'. It can be used as a rub for meat or fish to be cooked on the barbecue, as a seasoning for rice, or as a basic spice blend for most Lebanese dishes. You can increase the quantity to suit your needs.

---

3 tablespoons ground cinnamon

3 tablespoons freshly grated nutmeg

3 tablespoons ground black pepper

3 tablespoons ground allspice

Combine all the ingredients and mix well.

NOTE

The spice blend can be stored in an airtight container for up to 2 weeks, but I would recommend making it up as required.

BASTOURMA RUB

MAKES 100 G (3½ OZ)

The easiest explanation for 'bastourma' is that it's the Middle Eastern version of pastrami. It's a very fragrant cured meat that is specific to the Mediterranean. This rub allows you to add the flavour of bastourma to dishes like grilled fish or meat. The fenugreek gives it its distinctive flavour and fragrance.

3 tablespoons ground fenugreek

3 tablespoons mild paprika

2 teaspoons salt

2 teaspoons ground black pepper

2 teaspoons ground cumin

2 teaspoons ground allspice

1 teaspoon cayenne pepper

3 garlic cloves

3 tablespoons olive oil

Combine all the ingredients in a bowl with 4 tablespoons water and mix to a paste. Add a little extra water, if needed.

Store the rub in an airtight container for up to 2 weeks.

CHERMOULA

MAKES 350 G (12 OZ)

Chermoula is a drier version of a curry paste. It works well with fish or seafood as the lemon gives it a lovely tanginess. You can also use the chermoula to marinate chicken or add it to a salad dressing or mayonnaise.

2 tablespoons cumin seeds

2 tablespoons coriander seeds

1 tablespoon caraway seeds

1 brown onion, coarsely chopped

4 garlic cloves

2 handfuls coriander (cilantro), leaves, stems and roots washed well

1 large fresh green chilli

1 preserved lemon, rind only

3 teaspoons ground turmeric

2½ tablespoons lemon juice

100 ml (3½ fl oz) olive oil

Heat a frying pan over medium heat and dry-fry the cumin, coriander and caraway seeds for about 3 minutes, or until fragrant. Using a food processor, break the seeds down until coarse.

Add the onion, garlic, coriander, chilli, preserved lemon rind and turmeric to the food processor. Blend to a smooth paste, then add the lemon juice and blend for a further 2 minutes.

Scrape down the side of the bowl. With the motor running, slowly drizzle in the olive oil. Season to taste.

Put the chermoula in a sterilised jar and seal. Store in the fridge for up to 2 weeks.

Pictured on page 222

HAZELNUT DUKKAH

MAKES 520 G (1 LB 2 OZ)

Dukkah is a versatile blend of spices. Mix it with some olive oil and serve it as a dip with warm bread. You can dust it on pieces of meat before barbecuing or sprinkle it over salads. The hazelnuts can be replaced with any nuts you like. I make a lovely sweet dukkah by replacing the salt with sugar and the spices with sweeter spices, such as cinnamon, nutmeg and cloves. Be creative!

250 g (9 oz/1¾ cups) hazelnuts

1 tablespoon coriander seeds

1 tablespoon cumin seeds

185 g (6½ oz/1¼ cups) sesame seeds

2 teaspoons sea salt flakes

2 teaspoons freshly ground black pepper

Preheat the oven to 160°C (315°F).

Put the hazelnuts on one baking tray, and the coriander and cumin seeds on a separate tray, and bake for approximately 15 minutes, or until toasted.

After the hazelnuts and seeds have been in the oven for 10 minutes, add the sesame seeds on a separate tray and toast for the remaining 5 minutes, or until lightly coloured. Remove all the trays from the oven and allow the nuts and seeds to cool to room temperature.

Put the hazelnuts in a food processor and pulse to a coarse breadcrumb size. (You could also crush the hazelnuts the traditional way using a mortar and pestle—good exercise for the biceps!) Transfer the hazelnuts to a large bowl.

Put the cumin and coriander seeds in the food processor and process until almost a powder. (You can do this using a mortar and pestle if you prefer.)

Add this powder to the bowl along with the toasted sesame seeds, salt and pepper. Mix well using a wooden spoon.

Dukkah can be kept for up to 1 year—but I am sure you will eat it all before then! It's best stored in an airtight container in a cool, dry place.

Pictured on page 209

GREEN ZHOUG

MAKES 600 G (1 LB 5 OZ)

Zhoug is like a Middle Eastern version of gremolata. It can be used as a substitute for chilli—it has a little more flavour and a lot more kick.

15 large fresh green chillies, chopped

10 garlic cloves

1 large handful coriander (cilantro), leaves and stems chopped

1 large handful flat-leaf (Italian) parsley, chopped

250 ml (9 fl oz/1 cup) olive oil

Put the chilli, garlic, coriander and parsley in a food processor and blend to a paste. Add the olive oil, season with salt and blitz to combine.

Spoon the mixture into a sterilised jar. Store in the fridge for up to 2 weeks.

MATBUCHA

FILLS A 1 LITRE (35 FL OZ/4 CUP) JAR

Let's not argue about the origins of matbucha—some claim it's from Libya, others Morocco and even Turkey. I say it's from our fridge and it's delicious. Matbucha is fantastic warm or cold, as a lovely relish over bread and cold cuts. It can be eaten as a salad and actually 'warm salad' is its literal translation from Arabic. I have also seen people using it as a base for shakshuka. At Kepos Street Kitchen we use matbucha in a main course dish of ocean trout moussaka.

———

4 tablespoons light olive oil

1 small brown onion, finely chopped

6 garlic cloves, finely chopped

1 large capsicum (pepper), cut into 1 cm (½ inch) dice

2 large fresh green chillies, chopped

12 small to medium tomatoes, peeled and cut into 1 cm (½ inch) dice, or 2 x 400 g (14 oz) tins chopped tomatoes

3 tablespoons sweet paprika

1 tablespoon ground coriander

1 tablespoon ground cumin

1 teaspoon salt

1 teaspoon sugar

1½ tablespoons extra virgin olive oil

Heat the light olive oil in a frying pan over medium heat. Add the onion and garlic and cook for 5 minutes, or until transparent but not coloured. Add the capsicum and chilli and cook for 5–7 minutes, until softened without breaking up. Add the tomato, reduce the heat to medium–low and cook for 30 minutes, or until reduced by half.

Stir in the paprika, coriander, cumin, salt and sugar and cook for a further 5 minutes. Add the extra virgin olive oil and cook for 1 minute. Remove the pan from the heat and allow to cool.

Spoon the matbucha into a sterilised jar and store in the fridge for up to 5 days.

CHAPTER EIGHT

PICKLES PRESERVES, STOCKS & BASICS

This chapter contains basic recipes and techniques that are used throughout the book. Pickling is a great way to make the most of seasonal ingredients and it's also a very loose and intuitive way to cook because you can adjust the flavours to your liking.

Other recipes here, like the pizza dough, are great foundation recipes to build on. Once you've mastered them, the variations and things you can make are endless. Homemade stocks add depth to your dishes and they freeze well so you can always have them on hand for extra nutrition and flavour.

PICKLED GREEN TOMATOES

FILLS A 1.5 LITRE (52 FL OZ/6 CUP) JAR

Pickling is a great way to preserve your favourite vegetables, especially when they are in season—at their cheapest but also at their best. Green tomatoes sustain their crunch and texture and make a lovely addition to sandwiches.

Put the vinegar and salt in a large saucepan along with 600 ml (21 fl oz) of water and bring to the boil.

Put the tomato, spices, chilli, dill, garlic and bay leaves in a 2 litre (70 fl oz/8 cup) sterilised jar. Pour in the hot liquid and seal. Place the jar in a dark place (the back of a cupboard is ideal) for 3 weeks.

After 3 weeks, the pickled tomatoes are ready to eat. Once opened, store the jar in the fridge for up to 4 to 5 weeks.

600 ml (21 fl oz) white vinegar

1 tablespoon salt

750 g (1 lb 10 oz) green tomatoes, halved or thickly sliced

1 tablespoon coriander seeds

1 tablespoon cumin seeds

2 teaspoons black peppercorns

2 large fresh green chillies, halved lengthways

5 dill sprigs

4 garlic cloves, lightly crushed

5 bay leaves

PRESERVED TUNA

MAKES 250 G (9 OZ)

Making your own preserves is very rewarding and you can control the ingredients and flavours. I like to use bay leaves and peppercorns when I'm preserving tuna, but you could add lemon zest, garlic, chilli or any other flavouring you like. This tuna is the hero ingredient in Tunisian tuna salad (page 83).

Put the piece of tuna in a small saucepan and add the oil, bay leaves and peppercorns. Bring to a simmer or light bubble (it shouldn't be boiling) and cook for 10 minutes. Remove the pan from the heat and set aside to cool.

Carefully transfer the piece of tuna to a sterilised jar. Pour in the olive oil, bay leaves and peppercorns and seal the jar. Store the preserved tuna in the fridge for up to 2 weeks.

250 g (9 oz) piece tuna loin
625 ml (21½ fl oz/2½ cups) olive oil
3 bay leaves
5 black peppercorns

SPICY NUTS

MAKES 300 G (10½ OZ)

Growing up, my mum always had containers of nuts in the pantry for when guests dropped in unexpectedly, which would happen pretty frequently. Mum would make these spicy nuts that were a bit too spicy for us kids, but now I'm addicted to them and like to have them at my house.

Preheat the oven to 170°C (340°F). Line a large baking tray with baking paper.

Put all the ingredients in a bowl and mix to combine. Spread the mixture over the baking tray and bake for 5–7 minutes, until lightly coloured. Stir the nuts halfway through cooking. Set aside to cool to room temperature.

The cooled nuts can be stored in an airtight container for up to 2 weeks—if they last that long!

75 g (2½ oz/½ cup) almonds

75 g (2½ oz/½ cup) hazelnuts

75 g (2½ oz/½ cup) cashews

75 g (2½ oz/½ cup) macadamia nuts

1 teaspoon cayenne pepper

½ teaspoon ground cumin

1 tablespoon sugar

1 teaspoon sea salt flakes

4 tablespoons olive oil

PICKLED LEBANESE-STYLE BABY EGGPLANTS

FILLS A 1 LITRE (35 FL OZ/4 CUP) JAR

I was introduced to these pickles by a Lebanese friend of mine. His mother used to make them for him here in Australia. I was intrigued by their amazing, intense flavour. These eggplants are an excellent addition to your mezze table.

Cut off and discard the eggplant tops. Thoroughly wash the eggplants, then put them in a large saucepan and cover with cold water. Cover the eggplants with a plate to keep them submerged. Bring to the boil, then cook over medium heat for 15 minutes. Drain and allow to cool to room temperature.

Cover a baking tray with a tea towel (dish towel). Cut a slit in the side of each eggplant, open it out flat and place it on the tray. Put another tea towel on top and press down with a weight. Set the eggplants aside overnight, or for at least 8 hours. This will remove any excess water.

Chop the walnuts until they are roughly the size of grains of rice. Mix with the garlic, salt, pomegranate molasses, coriander and chilli flakes. Stuff the mixture into the slit in the eggplants. Put a layer of eggplants in the bottom of a sterilised jar and sprinkle with some paprika. Add the remaining eggplants, sprinkling with more paprika and adding 1 tablespoon of the red wine vinegar after every three eggplants. Pour in enough of the olive oil to fill the jar and seal. Place the jar in a dark place (the back of a cupboard is ideal) for 3 weeks.

After 3 weeks, the pickled eggplants are ready to eat. Once opened, store in the fridge for up to 2 weeks.

1 kg (2 lb 4 oz) baby eggplants (aubergines), preferably purple, not green

100 g (3½ oz) walnuts

6 garlic cloves, crushed

2 tablespoons rock salt

3 tablespoons pomegranate molasses

1 handful coriander (cilantro), leaves and stems finely chopped

1 tablespoon chilli flakes

1 tablespoon sweet paprika

3 tablespoons red wine vinegar

250 ml (9 fl oz/1 cup) olive oil, approximately

BEEF STOCK

MAKES ABOUT 2 LITRES (70 FL OZ/8 CUPS)

Most people enjoy the convenience of commercial stocks, but if you have time to make it, homemade stock makes such a difference to the end result.

1 kg (2 lb 4 oz) beef bones

3 tablespoons light olive oil

2 small carrots, coarsely chopped

2 brown onions, coarsely chopped

2 celery stalks, coarsely chopped

250 ml (9 fl oz/1 cup) red wine (optional)

6 black peppercorns

2 fresh bay leaves

6 flat-leaf (Italian) parsley stalks

2 thyme sprigs

Preheat the oven to 200°C (400°F).

Put the beef bones on a large baking tray and roast for 25–30 minutes, until the bones have browned. Set aside.

Heat the olive oil in a large saucepan over high heat. Add the carrot, onion and celery and cook for 5–7 minutes, until the vegetables are golden brown. Add the wine, if using, and cook until reduced by half.

Add the beef bones, peppercorns, bay leaves, parsley, thyme and 4 litres (140 fl oz/16 cups) of water to the pan and bring to the boil. Reduce the heat to medium–low and simmer, skimming occasionally, for 2½–3 hours.

Strain the stock, discarding the bones, vegetables and aromatics. Store in the fridge for up to 1 week or in the freezer for up to 2 months.

CHICKEN STOCK

MAKES ABOUT 2 LITRES (70 FL OZ/8 CUPS)

Chicken stock is the most commonly used stock in recipes. It really doesn't take much effort to make and it's always good to have it in the freezer. My mum says that chicken stock has healing benefits. I'm not sure if that's true, but I will continue believing that it is and I will try to convince you, too!

1 kg (2 lb 4 oz) chicken bones or chicken carcasses, washed

1 large carrot, coarsely chopped

2 small brown onions, coarsely chopped

2 celery stalks, coarsely chopped

5 flat-leaf (Italian) parsley stalks

6 black peppercorns

3 thyme sprigs

4 garlic cloves

Combine all the ingredients in a large saucepan and add 4 litres (140 fl oz/16 cups) of water. Bring to the boil over high heat, then reduce the heat to medium–low and simmer, skimming occasionally, for 1½–2 hours.

Strain the stock, discarding the bones, vegetables and aromatics. Store in the fridge for up to 4 days or in the freezer for up to 2 months.

VEGETABLE STOCK

MAKES ABOUT 2 LITRES (70 FL OZ/8 CUPS)

Making your own vegetable stock is really very simple and inexpensive. As with all homemade stocks, it gives an intense flavour to your dishes. It's also a great way to impress your vegan friends.

3 tablespoons olive oil

2 brown onions, coarsely chopped

2 large carrots, coarsely chopped

3 celery stalks, coarsely chopped

1 small leek, coarsely chopped

5 flat-leaf (Italian) parsley stalks

6 black peppercorns

3 bay leaves

Heat the oil in a large saucepan over medium heat. Sauté the onion, carrot, celery and leek for 3–5 minutes, until the vegetables are softened but not coloured.

Add the parsley stalks, peppercorns, bay leaves and 3 litres (105 fl oz/12 cups) of water and bring to the boil. Reduce the heat to medium–low and simmer, skimming occasionally if needed, for 1½–2 hours.

Strain the stock, discarding the vegetables and aromatics. Store in the fridge for up to 1 week or in the freezer for up to 2 months.

FISH STOCK

MAKES ABOUT 2 LITRES (70 FL OZ/8 CUPS)

It can be hard to find commercial fish stock. If you are using fish stock in a recipe, I highly recommend that you make your own.

3 tablespoons olive oil

1 large brown onion, coarsely chopped

2 small carrots, coarsely chopped

3 celery stalks, coarsely chopped

½ leek, coarsely chopped

250 ml (9 fl oz/1 cup) white wine (optional)

1 kg (2 lb 4 oz) fish bones, preferably from white fish

6 white peppercorns

5 flat-leaf (Italian) parsley stalks

3 bay leaves

Heat the olive oil in a large saucepan over medium heat. Sauté the onion, carrot, celery and leek for 2–3 minutes. Add the wine, if using, and cook for 4–5 minutes, until reduced by half.

Add the fish bones, peppercorns, parsley, bay leaves and 3 litres (105 fl oz/12 cups) of water. Increase the heat to high and bring to the boil. Reduce the heat to medium–low and simmer, skimming occasionally, for 1½–2 hours.

Strain the stock, discarding the bones, vegetables and aromatics. Store in the fridge for up to 5 days or in the freezer for up to 2 months.

PIZZA DOUGH

MAKES 8 X 125 G (4½ OZ) BALLS PIZZA DOUGH

Once you have mastered this recipe, it is very easy to make your own dough each time you feel like pizza and you will never want to order takeaway pizza again. This dough is best used within 2 hours of preparation and I don't recommend freezing it.

Using an electric mixer fitted with a hook attachment, mix the yeast, sugar and warm water until the yeast and sugar have dissolved. Reduce the speed to low and add the oil, then add the flour and mix until the dough comes together as a soft ball. This will take about 5 minutes. Add the salt and mix for a further 2–3 minutes (adding the salt last means it won't slow down the yeast). The dough should not be too firm or too wet.

Transfer the dough onto a lightly floured board. Divide the dough into 8 balls and put them on a large baking tray lined with baking paper. Wring out a wet tea towel (dish towel) and use it to cover the dough balls. Leave the dough balls to rise for 1 hour, or until they have doubled in size.

To shape the dough, lightly flour a dough ball all over. Holding the dough with both hands, work around the dough, carefully stretching it in a circular motion and taking care not to tear it. Shape the dough so that the centre is thinner than the crust.

14 g (½ oz) dried yeast

1 tablespoon caster (superfine) sugar

500 ml (17 fl oz/2 cups) warm water

50 ml (1½ fl oz) olive oil

1 kg (2 lb 4 oz) 00 flour or plain (all-purpose) flour, plus extra for dusting

1 tablespoon salt

SWEET SHORTCRUST PASTRY

MAKES A 24 CM (9½ INCH) TART BASE

Great pastry counts for fifty per cent of your dessert, especially when it comes to pies and tarts. It can take a while to perfect homemade pastry, so don't give up! Although there are some good-quality commercial pastries, always try to make your own—it's worth the effort.

Using an electric mixer fitted with a paddle attachment, mix the butter, icing sugar and vanilla extract until light and fluffy. Scrape down the side of the bowl, then add the lemon zest and egg yolk and beat for 1 minute. Fold in the sifted flour until combined, being careful not to overwork the mixture.

Cover the pastry with plastic wrap and rest in the fridge for at least 2 hours before using.

100 g (3½ oz) unsalted butter, at room temperature
50 g (1¾ oz) icing (confectioners') sugar
½ teaspoon natural vanilla extract
grated zest of ½ lemon
1 egg yolk
150 g (5½ oz/1 cup) plain (all-purpose) flour, sifted

MAYONNAISE

MAKES ABOUT 600 G (1 LB 5 OZ)

Mayonnaise is a versatile recipe and you can add almost any ingredient you like to flavour it. To make aïoli, roast 10 garlic cloves in some olive oil and add them to the food processor with the egg yolks, mustard and vinegar.

Put the egg yolks, mustard and vinegar in a food processor and blitz until combined, about 30 seconds. With the motor running, slowly drizzle in the combined vegetable and olive oils. This will take about 4-5 minutes.

Scrape down the side of the bowl. Add the lemon juice and season with salt, to taste. Mix with a spatula until combined.

Store in an airtight container in the fridge for up to 1 week.

2 egg yolks
1 tablespoon dijon mustard
1½ tablespoons white wine vinegar
250 ml (9 fl oz/1 cup) vegetable oil
250 ml (9 fl oz/1 cup) olive oil
juice of ½ lemon

SUGAR SYRUP

MAKES 750 ML (26 FL OZ/3 CUPS)

Sugar syrup can be used in cocktails, mocktails and other drinks such as coffee and iced tea. At the restaurants, we use raw (demerara) sugar to make sugar syrup because of the lovely flavour of sugarcane molasses, but you can use basically any type of sugar you have.

Put the sugar in a large heatproof bowl with a lip. Pour in the freshly boiled water and stir until the sugar has dissolved. Allow to cool, then pour into a bottle.

Store the syrup in the fridge for up to 1 month.

500 g (1 lb 2 oz) raw (demerara) sugar

500 ml (17 fl oz/2 cups) boiling water

HOW TO SEGMENT CITRUS

This is a great technique to use to segment fruit for the Orange, harissa and black olive salad (page 65) as well as segmenting the grapefruit for the Layered Turkish delight pavlova (page 183).

Cut off the top and bottom of the citrus fruit. Using a sharp knife, carefully remove the skin and white pith, following the line of the fruit. Remove each segment by slicing either side of the membrane. It is good to do this over a bowl to capture any juice that comes out of the fruit.

ACKNOWLEDGMENTS

A MASSIVE THANK YOU TO EVERYONE INVOLVED IN OUR COOKBOOK.

To our families who have always been supportive, keep us laughing, evolving and are always happy to come over to our house for a meal.

Thank you to Terry Durack and Jill Dupleix for inviting us back for seconds. We are flattered that you felt the world needed to see more recipes from us. It was great brainstorming ideas with you over a Kepos lunch box.

The team at Murdoch Books has been amazing to work with again. Thank you Sue Hines for believing in us a second time around as well. And Lou Johnson for taking over where Sue left off. Murdoch Books have allowed us an amazing freedom with this book. Corinne Roberts has been a guiding light throughout, always there to bounce off ideas, offer suggestions and comments and most importantly give feedback with our recipe testing! Glad we were able to combine meetings with a tasty lunch. Thank you to Viv Valk for visualising our ideas. We really should have caught up for coffee rather than our long phone calls. Thanks Katie Bosher for taking the flatplan and creating a workable shoot, managing the whole editorial process and all round general co-ordination of the pages that come together to make this book. To Murray Batten for creating the most beautiful pages with a design and colour palette that complement our food but also us. Thanks as well to Justine Harding, our recipe editor, for tweaking and correcting the recipes. Sorry for all the scribble with our answers on the manuscript. It takes so many people to bring an idea to life and this has been a great team to work with.

Alan Benson. What can we say? We have so much fun working with you. Those two weeks felt more like time spent with a friend rather than just hard work. It's amazing that you have a different lens for every dish! You are creative and extremely passionate and that reflects in the beautiful images. We love these photos.

Our amazing stylist Berni Smithies. There was no need for a brief as you get our food, our style and our vision. You allowed us freedom of expression and to put in our two cents' worth, even though we always went back to your suggestion. Working with you was an absolute pleasure. With the styling and photography, it was truly a creative collaboration. Thank you as well to Design Tiles, who loaned us their beautiful tiles for the shoot.

It was amazing this time round to have help in the kitchen during the shoots, so we owe a big thank you to Ross Dobson and Claire Dickson-Smith. Thanks for all the shopping, prepping and cooking. Made our life much, much easier.

Ladi Smid, our very talented beverage manager: thanks for your input in the tea chapter. You are always so creative, innovative and full of new ideas. All we need to do is brief you once on the subject and off you go. Thanks for the time spent on developing the recipes with us.

Thanks to the team at both Kepos Street Kitchen and Kepos & Co. In particular the main characters who backed us up at work, allowing us the time to work on this book. From Kepos Street Kitchen—Roy Chason, Sujan Shretha, Everton Martins, Kaili Vaard and Sada Fletcher. From Kepos & Co—Artur and Yulia Bilder, Nicola Basnakova and Ladi Smid.

We've hosted a lot of people while working on this cookbook, so thanks to all our taste testers. Hope that job wasn't too bad.

Thank you to Diane and Peter Frawley for the lovely words in the introduction. You are the foundation of our family. With Michael's parents so far away, you are always there for him; supportive and passionate about everything we do.

MICHAEL RANTISSI & KRISTY FRAWLEY

INDEX

Published in 2017 by Murdoch Books, an imprint of Allen & Unwin

Murdoch Books Australia
83 Alexander Street
Crows Nest NSW 2065
Phone: +61 (0) 2 8425 0100
Fax: +61 (0) 2 9906 2218
murdochbooks.com.au
info@murdochbooks.com.au

Murdoch Books UK
Ormond House
26–27 Boswell Street
London WC1N 3JZ
Phone: +44 (0) 20 8785 5995
murdochbooks.co.uk
info@murdochbooks.co.uk

For Corporate Orders & Custom Publishing, contact our Business
Development Team at salesenquiries@murdochbooks.com.au

Publisher: Corinne Roberts
Editorial Manager: Katie Bosher
Design Manager: Vivien Valk
Project Editor: Justine Harding
Designer: Murray Batten
Photographer: Alan Benson
Stylist: Berni Smithies
Home Economists: Ross Dobson & Claire Dickson-Smith
Production Manager: Lou Playfair

A cataloguing-in-publication entry is available from the catalogue of the
National Library of Australia at nla.gov.au.

ISBN 978 1 76052 263 6 Australia
ISBN 978 1 76052 765 5 UK

A catalogue record for this book is available from the British Library.

Colour reproduction by Splitting Image Colour Studio Pty Ltd,
Clayton, Victoria

Printed by 1010 Printing International Limited, China

IMPORTANT: Those who might be at risk from the effects of salmonella
poisoning (the elderly, pregnant women, young children and those
suffering from immune deficiency diseases) should consult their doctor
with any concerns about eating raw eggs.

OVEN GUIDE: You may find cooking times vary depending on the oven you
are using. For fan-forced ovens, as a general rule, set the oven temperature
to 20°C (70°F) lower than indicated in the recipe.

MEASURES GUIDE: We have used 20 ml (4 teaspoon) tablespoon measures.
If you are using a 15 ml (3 teaspoon) tablespoon add an extra teaspoon of
the ingredient for each tablespoon specified.